Encountering God in Genesis

Brenda Frost

Encountering God in Genesis

This book is written to provide information and motivation to readers. Its purpose is not to render any type of psychological, legal, or professional advice of any kind. The content is the sole opinion and expression of the author, and not necessarily that of the publisher.

Copyright © 2020 by Brenda Frost

All rights reserved. No part of this book may be reproduced, transmitted, or distributed in any form by any means, including, but not limited to, recording, photocopying, or taking screenshots of parts of the book, without prior written permission from the author or the publisher. Brief quotations for noncommercial purposes, such as book reviews, permitted by Fair Use of the U.S. Copyright Law, are allowed without written permissions, as long as such quotations do not cause damage to the book's commercial value. For permissions, write to the publisher, whose address is stated below.

Printed in the United States of America.

ISBN 978-1-953150-06-6 (Paperback)
ISBN 978-1-953150-07-3 (Digital)

Lettra Press books may be ordered through booksellers or by contacting:

Lettra Press LLC
30 N Gould St. Suite 4753
Sheridan, WY 82801, USA
1 307-200-3414 | info@lettrapress.com
www.lettrapress.com

With deepest love and appreciation, I dedicate this book to

Michaelene Lampshire

You are always there for me in the good times and the bad. You always encourage me. You are the best friend anyone could ask for and a true blessing. I am so grateful to have you in my life.

Table of Contents

Introduction vii
WEEK ONE Creation 1
WEEK TWO Adam and Eve 23
WEEK THREE Mankind's Downward Spiral 55
WEEK FOUR Genesis 6-9 The Flood 77
WEEK FIVE 107
WEEK SIX 139
WEEK SEVEN Isaac 171
WEEK EIGHT Jacob 197
WEEK NINE 217
WEEK TEN 241
WEEK ELEVEN 257
Bibliography 273

Introduction

In the Book of Genesis we are introduced to God, the Creator of everything. Throughout the book, we learn many things about God as He interacts with and reveals Himself to His creation. In this book we see God interacting with many people, those who believe and know God, such as Adam and Eve, Cain, Noah, Abraham, Isaac, Jacob, and Joseph, and those who don't know God such as Pharaoh and Hagar.

The Book of Genesis is quoted or referred to more than 100 times in the New Testament, and by Jesus Himself. Genesis is the foundation of the entire Bible. Therefore understanding Genesis is crucial to understanding the rest of Scripture.

Because many of the stories of Genesis are familiar, it is easy to just skim over them and miss much of the rich lessons that can be found in them. From this book we can learn many lessons about relating to God as well as family relations and lessons for living every day life. This guide is designed to get the reader to dig in deeper to gain new insights and principles.

This study is organized into eleven weeks, which are divided into five days of studies. The study is divided into several different sections.

In the section titled **Observation** are questions based on the text which is being studied.

The section titled **Correlation** we will look at other texts in the Bible which cover topics found in the section which we are looking at.

There will be a brief **Commentary** given.

Under **Vocabulary** we will cover the meaning of important words.

Under **Application** there will be questions that will apply what we've studied to our personal lives.

I hope that this study will help you to mine the gems which the Bible contains for living our lives.

In Genesis are portraits of the Patriarchs from which many lessons can be learned.

We are told in **1 Corinthians 10:6,11** These things happened as a warning to us, so that we would not crave evil things as they did,... These things happened to them as examples for us. They were written down to warn us who live at the end of the age. We are also told in **Romans 15:4** Such things were written in the Scriptures long ago to teach us. And the Scriptures give us hope and encouragement as we wait patiently for God's promises to be fulfilled. From these people we can learn positive lessons such as faith, obedience, forgiveness, as well as things we should avoid, such as anger, hatred, and vengence.

The Bible is God's love letter to us. In it we find many principles for living life the way God intended for us to live. The Bible is life's instruction book. If we live by it we will find life better than if we go our own way.

May God speak to you and bless you as you spend time with His Word.

WEEK ONE
Creation

GENESIS 1-2: 3

DAY ONE

INTRODUCTION TO GENESIS

Title

The first three words in the English text of **Genesis 1:1** is the Hebrew word bereshith ("in [the] beginning"), which is also the Hebrew title of the book (books in ancient times customarily were named after their first word or two). The English title, Genesis, is Greek in origin and comes from the word geneseos, which appears in the Greek translation (Septuagint) of **2:4; 5:1**. Depending on its context, the word can mean "birth," "genealogy," or "history of origin." In both its Hebrew and Greek form, the title of Genesis is a good description of its contents, since it is a book of beginnings.

The Septuagint is the earliest known Greek translation of the Hebrew Scriptures, which originated in Egypt between 300 and 200 BC.

Its name means "seventy" in Latin and is derived from the belief that seventy-two scholars worked on its production.

Author and Date of Writing

These books are also known as the Pentateuch which means "five-volumed book"; *penta* means five, *teuchos* means scroll or book.

Historically, Jews and Christians alike have held that Moses was the author/compiler of the first five books of the OT.

Roman historian Josephus stated that Moses was the author.

Jesus also attributed the writings of these books to Moses.

> "But do not think I will accuse you before the Father. Your accuser is Moses, on whom your hopes are set. 46 If you believed Moses, you would believe me, for he wrote about me. 47But since you do not believe what he wrote, how are you going to believe what I say?" ***John 5:45-47***

Although there is no author's name given in the book, there are allusions to Moses being the author within the Pentateuch.

> Then the LORD said to Moses, "Write this on a scroll as something to be remembered and make sure that Joshua hears it, because I will completely blot out the memory of Amalek from under heaven." ***Exodus 17:14***

> Moses then wrote down everything the LORD had said. ***Exodus 24:4***

> Then he took the Book of the Covenant and read it to the people. ***Exodus 24:7***

> At the LORD's command Moses recorded the stages in their journey. ***Numbers 33:2***

The period during which Moses lived seems to be fixed with a fair degree of accuracy by **1 Kings.** We are told that "the fourth year of Solomon's reign over Israel was the same as the four hundred and eightieth year after the Israelites had come out of Egypt" (**1Ki 6:1**). Since the former was c. 966 BC, the latter—and thus the date of the exodus—was c. 1446 . The forty-year period of Israel's wanderings in the desert, which lasted from c. 1446 to c.1406, would have been the most likely time for Moses to write the bulk of what is today known as the Pentateuch.

Theme

Moses wrote the book for the Israelites who were entering the Promised Land.

The book of Genesis is foundational to the understanding of the rest of the Bible. In it we find the beginning of everything, from creation of the world to the first sin, first murder, first promise of salvation. It documents the beginning of God's interaction with man, which is continued throughout the Bible.

It is ultimately a book of relationships, highlighting those between God and nature, God and people, and people with each other .

It clearly teaches that the one true God is sovereign over all that exists (i.e., His entire creation), and that by divine choice He often exercises His authority to overturn human customs, traditions and plans.

Many subjects are covered in the book. Many of the sciences are found in this book. For example:

Science-The origin of the universe is found in Genesis.

History- Genesis describes the beginnings of civilization and the origins of the Israelites.

Theology-In Genesis we begin to learn about the nature and character of God, such as His holiness and His faithfulness. We also see God is the only and sovereign ruler of the universe. We see Him as the Creator and sustainer of all life. He is the judge of all the earth-(see Genesis 18:25)

*Psychology and Sociology-*In Genesis we see dysfunctional families and different aspects of human nature such as anger and jealousy.

Genesis covers a time span of approximately 4,200 years. Joseph died about 1800 B.C. The whole rest of the OT covers only about 1,100 years.

The New Testament, excluding the book of Revelation, covers about one hundred years, -from the birth of Jesus to the beginnings of the early church at the end of the first century.

Geography

The geographical area of the first eleven chapters is in the area of the Fertile Crescent. The setting of the chapters covering the patriarchs is the land of Canaan.

Outline:

I. Primeval History (**1:1-11:26**)

    A. Creation (**1:1-2:3**)
        1. World
        2. Universe
        3. Living Organisms-Plants and animals
        4. Humans

    B. Adam and Eve in Eden (**2:4-25**)

    C. The fall and Its consequences (**chapter 3**)
        1. Rebellion
        2. Results of sin
            a. Fear

       b. Broken relationships
          i. Between Adam and Eve
          ii. Between people and God
       c. Consequences of Sin
          i. Death of innocent animal
          ii. Expulsion from Eden
          iii. Gods judgment

D. Cain and Abel (**4:1-16**)
   1. Sibling Rivalry (**4:1-7**)
   2. The first murder (**4:8**)
   3. Judgment pronounced (**4:9-15**)

E. Two genealogies (**4:17-5:32**)
   1. The genealogy of Cain (**4:17-24**)
   2. The genealogy of Seth (**4:25-5:32**)

F. The flood (**6-9**)
   1. God's decision
      a. Judgment of the ungodly (**6:3-7**)
      b. Grace shown to Noah (**6:8**)
   2. The flood
      a. Preparations made (**6:13-22**)
      b. Entering the ark (**7:1-10**)
      c. The flood comes (**7:11-24**)
      d. Waters recede (**8:1-14**)
      e. Leaving the ark (**8:15-19**)
   3. The floods aftermath (**8:20-9:29**)
      a. New promise (**8:20-22**)
      b. New ordinances (**9:1-7**)
      c. New relationship (**9:8-17**)
      d. Sons of Noah (**9:18-19**)
      e. Ham's disrespect and resulting curse (**9:20-27**)
      f. Noah's death (**9:28-29**)

    G.   The spread of the nations (**10:1-32**)
            1.   Family of Japheth (**10:1-5**)
            2.   Family of Ham (**10:6-14**)
            3.   Family of Canaan (**10:15-20**)
            4.   Family of Shem (**10:21-32**)

    H.   The Tower of Babel
            1.   Construction of the tower (**11:1-4**)
            2.   The confusion of tongues (**11:5-9**)
            3.   The first Semitic genealogy (**11:10-26**)

II.   Patriarchal History (**11:27-50:26**)

    A.   The life of Abraham (**11:27-25:11**)
            1.   Abraham's background (**11:27-32**)
            2.   Abraham's call (**12:1-3**)
                a.   Abrahams response (**12:4-9**)

            3.   Abraham in Egypt (**12:10-20**)
            4.   Abraham and Lot (**12-14**)
            5.   Ratification of the covenant (**15**)
                a.   Promise of children (**15:1-5**)
                b.   Abraham's faith (**15:6**)
                c.   Covenant ceremony (**15:9-12,17-18**)
                d.   Prophecy of four hundred year affliction of descendants (**15:13-16**)
                e.   Promise of land (**15:7,18-21**)

            6.   Abraham and Hagar (**16**)
            7.   Covenant of circumcision (**17**)
            8.   Abraham intercedes for Sodom and Gomorrah (**18:16-33**)
            9.   Destruction of Sodom and Gomorrah (**19**)
                a.   Mercy shown to Lot (**19:1-29**)
                b.   Lot's depravity (**19:30-38**)

10. Abraham and Abimelech (**20**)
11. Birth of Isaac
    a. Prophesied (**18:1-15**)
    b. Birth (**21:1-8**)

12. Hagar and Ishmael expelled (**21:9-21**)
13. Abraham's obedience (**22**)
14. Death of Sarah (**23**)
15. Abraham remarries (**25:1-6**)
16. Abraham's death (**25:7-11**)

B. The descendants of Ishmael (**25:12-18**)

C. Isaac
   1. Marriage (**24**)
   2. Children (**25**)
   3. Abimelech (**26**)

D. The life of Jacob (**25:19-33; 27:1-35:29**)
   1. Birth of Jacob and Esau (**25:19-26**)
   2. Esau sells His Birthright (**25:27-34**)
       a. Jacob and Rebekah deceive Isaac (**27**)

   3. Jacob abroad (**28-30**)
       a. Jacobs Dream (**28:10-22**)
       b. Jacob and Laban (**29-31**)
       c. Jacob Wrestles With God (**32:22-30**)
       d. d. Facing Esau (**32:1-21;331-16**)

   4. Jacob at home again (**31-35**)
       a. Rape of Dinah (**34**)
       b. Death of Rachel (**35:16-20**)
       c. Death of Isaac (**35:27-29**)

E. The descendants of Esau (**36:1-37:1**)

F. Judah and Tamar (**39**)

G. The life of Joseph (**37:2-50:26**)
   1. Joseph and his brothers (**37:2-33**)
   2. Joseph in Egypt (**37:36; 39-50**)
      a. Joseph and Pontiphar (**39:1-6**)
      b. Joseph and Pontiphar's wife (**39:6-19**)
      c. Joseph in prison (**39:20-40:23**)
      d. Joseph interprets Pharoahs dreams (**41:1-36**)
      e. Joseph Promoted to Second in Command of Egypt (**41:37-48**)
      f. Josephs Marriage and Children (**41:45,50-51**)
      g. Josephs Dealings with His Brothers (**42-45**)
   3. Jacob reunited with Joseph (**46**)
   4. Jacob in Egypt (**47**)
   5. Jacobs last days (**48:1-50:14**)
      a. Jacobs blessing (**48:1-49:28**)
      b. Jacobs burial (**49:29-50:13**)
   6. Joseph's last days (**50:15-26**)

Day Two

CREATION

Observation-Genesis 1:1-Genesis 2:3

1. a. What does the word *Genesis* mean?
   b. What is the book of Genesis about?

2. Who was the author of Genesis?

3. When was Genesis written?

4. a. Who are we introduced to in **Genesis 1:1**?
   b. What are we told He did in this verse?
   c. When did He do this according to this verse?

5. What was the state of the earth before God acted?

6. What does **verse 2** state was hovering over the waters?

7. What did God create to divide the waters from the waters?

8. How were the limits of each day defined?

9. On what day of creation did God cause the dry land to appear?

10. What was created on each day?
    a. Day 1
    b. Day 2
    c. Day 3
    d. Day 4
    e. Day 5
    f. Day 6

11. a. What method did God use to create? See also **Psalm 33:6,9.**
    b. Compare **Genesis 1:1** with **John 1:1**.
    c. Who was the Word According to John? See also **John 1:3,14.**

12. What three things did God separate?

13. What things did God name?

14. a. When were the sun and moon created?

    b. What was the source of light in **verse 3**? See **Revelation 21:23**.

15. What was the purpose of the lights in the sky according to **verse 14**?

16. a. What was different about the creation of man from the rest of creation?
    b. In whose image was man made?
    c. What does this mean?

17. How is God referred to in **verse 26**?

18. What five instructions were given to Adam in **verse 28**?

19. a. What was God's pronouncement after each creative act?
    b. What was God's pronouncement on the sixth day?

20. What was to be Adam's food?

21. What did the animals eat?

22. What do we learn about God from the creation account?

23. What should be our response to God?

24. Go through the text of chapters 1 and 2, and mark all the actions God performed.
    a. God created
    b. God said
    c. God separated
    d. God called (named)
    e. God saw
    f. God blessed
    g. God completed

h. God commanded
   i. God rested
   j. God formed (made)
   k. God planted
   l. God placed
   m. God caused

Correlation-Comparing Other texts

1. What does the Bible say about who was involved in the creation? See
   John 1:1-3
   Colossians 1:15-17
   Hebrews 1:1-2.

2. What can we learn about God from His creation? See
   Romans 1:19-20
   Psalm 19:1

3. How should we respond to God Who created us? See
   Psalm 33:8-9
   Psalm 96:1-12
   Psalm 148:1-5
   Revelation 4:11.

4. What do we learn about the Word in **John 1:1-3,14**?

5. We are told in **Genesis 1:3** that God created light.
   a. What are we told in **1 John 1:5**?
   b. What are we told about Jesus in **John 1:4,7**?
   c. What are we told God does in **2 Corinthians 4:6**?

6. What do we learn from **Isaiah 40:26** concerning the stars?

7. What are some instances we see in the Bible of the stars being signs of events? See **Joel 2:30-31; Matthew 2:1-2; 24:30.**

8. How should the fact that we are created in God's image affect the way we treat others? See **1 John 4:7-8,12**

9. What are we told in **Hebrews 4:9-11** concerning the Sabbath rest?

10. On the seventh day God rested. He didn't rest because He was tired, but because His work was completed. What do we learn from the following verses about the Lord?
Psalm 121:4
Isaiah 40:28

11. The Lord didn't create the world to be empty. What are we told in **Isaiah 45:18**?

Day Three

Commentary

vs 1 *In the beginning...*-Hebrew *bereshit*
 *heavens and the earth...*This refers to the entire universe.

This account is not meant to be a scientific account. It does not deal so much with the "how" as the "who". This is not meant to prove the existence of God. His existence is a fact that is to be taken as a given.

God's existence is proven through His activity.

The name for God used here is Elohim. The form of the word is plural, and indicates a plentitude of power and majesty.

God has no beginning. He is eternal, He has always existed and will always exist. He is self-existent. This is something our finite minds find hard to grasp.

God created... We are not told the details of *how* God created, only *that* He created.

Ex nihilo nihil fit- from nothing nothing comes. The universe exists so some cause must have produced it. It didn't produce itself. That would be like a tornado going through a junk yard and creating a Boeing 747.

We are told in **Hebrews 3:4** For every house is builded by some man; but he that built all things is God. God is the source of all that exists in the created world.

vs 3 God called... The act of naming something is to claim ownership.

vs 14-18 Sun and moon... remember that the original audience was the new nation of Israel, who was getting ready to cross into the Promised Land. The surrounding people in the land of Canaan worshipped the sun and the moon as gods. Here Moses states that they were created and what their purpose was.

vs 20-25 Each type of organism has its own DNA-its own unique structure and can only reproduce after their own kind. An apple tree can not produce tomatoes.

vs 22 This is the first use of the word bless.

vs 29 *I give you...* Here we see God's provision for His creation.

Word Wealth

The word translated *firmament* comes from a Hebrew word that means "to spread out".

The word *subdue* means to conquor or bring under subjection.

Eden means pleasure or delight.

Food For Thought

Evolution vs Creation There are two reasons why the earth could not have evolved as evolution proclaims. The first is the Second Law of Thermodynamics also known as the Law of entropy, which says that when left alone, any system will fall into a state of decline and decay, and will fall into disorder. Everything is proceeding from order to chaos, and is corrupting. We see examples of this when buildings or machines are not maintained, they deteriorate.

The second reason is the extreme complexity of organisms. Consider just the complexity of just one organ such as the eye. The likelihood of this evolving is as likely as a tornado going through a junkyard and creating a Bowing 747.

Fascinating Facts

The adult brain weighs about three pounds and handles the information of 1000 supercomputers. The fundamental unit within the brain is the neuron, or nerve cell. Each cell contains a nucleus and branching fibers called dendrites and axons. Our brain contains about 10 billion neurons. The total length of the nerve dendrites in an adult brain is over 100,000 miles. Every single neuronal cell within the brain contains a trillion atoms.[1]

An elm tree produces 1,584,000,000 seeds during its life cycle, each of which also can produce another elm that can produce a similar number of seeds.[2]

There are 300 billion stars in our Milky Way galaxy alone. In 1999, observations by NASA astronomers, using the Hubble Space Telescope, suggests that there are 125 billion galaxies in the universe. The star count as of July 2003 was 70 sextillion observable stars. (70,000,00 0,000,000,000,000,000) This was part of the world's largest galaxy survey, the Two -Degree Field Galaxy Redshift Survey.[3]

Day Four

Digging Deeper- lessons learned from the passage

A. *Six days of Creation.*

Were they actual 24 hour days?

The Hebrew word translated day is *yom* which when used throughout the rest of the Old Testament referred to a 24 hour period of time. This is also supported by the repetition of the phrase "morning and evening"

B. *There are four lessons taught in this text concerning God.*
    1. *God is Eternal*

Genesis 1:1 In the beginning God created... This verse introduces us to the key person of the entire Bible. From this verse we learn that God existed before the heavens and the earth and that He is the creator of them. Anne Graham Lotz states "The opening phrase of Genesis reveals the divine nature of God. In this statement two attributes of God's divine glory are revealed; He is greater than creation, and He is separate from creation."[4]

In this account there is no attempt to explain the origin of God. His existence is to be taken as a given-on faith. His existence is proven through His activity.

God has always existed. He is eternal. He has and always will exist. He has no beginning. God was before the beginning of the world. There was nothing before God.

2. *God created everything out of nothing*

The word for created used here in Hebrew is *bara* and means "to make out of nothing". It does not mean to reform something out of something else. He is the source of all that exists.

Hebrews 11:3 By faith we understand that the universe was formed at God's command, so that what is seen was not made out of what was visible.

3. *God is a God of order*

He created in an orderly manner, not haphazardly.

There is a pattern and organization to the creation.

Fill in the following chart.

Place created	Place filled
Day 1	Day 4
(Gen 1:3-5)	**(Gen 1:14-19)**
Day 2	Day 5
(Gen 1:6-8)	**(Gen 1:20-23)**
Day 3	Day 6
(Gen 1:9-13)	**(Gen 1:24-31)**

4. *God is sovereign and preeminent over His creation*

Because God created the universe, he is the sovereign ruler over it, and in control of it. God didn't create the universe and then walk away. He is continually acting on behalf of creation.

Sovereign means to "be above or superior to all others, to be greatest, supreme, independent of all others." God has the authority and ability to govern all things because He is the source-the Creator of all things.

Preeminent is to be surpassing or exell over others. It carries the idea of being dominant.

Some verses which speak of God's sovereignty:

> Although the whole earth is mine, **Exodus 19:5**

> To the LORD your God belong the heavens, even the highest heavens, the earth and everything in it. **Deuteronomy 10:14**

> for the LORD your God is God in heaven above and on the earth below. **Joshua 2:11**

> Yours, O LORD, is the greatness and the power and the glory and the majesty and the splendor, for everything in heaven and earth is yours. Yours, O LORD, is the kingdom; you are exalted as head over all. **1 Chronicles 29:11**

> "Dominion and awe belong to God; he establishes order in the heights of heaven. **Job 25:2**

> for dominion belongs to the LORD and he rules over the nations. **Psalm 22:28**

> The heavens are yours, and yours also the earth; you founded the world and all that is in it. **Psalm 89:11**

The LORD does whatever pleases him, in the heavens and on the earth, in the seas and all their depths.[7] He makes clouds rise from the ends of the earth; he sends lightning with the rain and brings out the wind from his storehouses. ***Psalm 135:6-7***

" `The decision is announced by messengers, the holy ones declare the verdict, so that the living may know that the Most High is sovereign over the kingdoms of men and gives them to anyone he wishes and sets over them the lowliest of men.' ***Daniel 4:17***

...acknowledge that the Most High is sovereign over the kingdoms of men and gives them to anyone he wishes. ***Daniel 4:25***

`For in him we live and move and have our being.' ***Acts 17:28***

C. *The Triune God*

Notice in **verse 26** that God says "let *us* make man in *our* image, after *our* likeness. This verse points to the Holy Trinity: Father, Son and Holy Spirit.

We see the three persons in **Matthew 3:16-17** where Jesus is baptized, the Holy Spirit descends like a dove upon Jesus, and the voice from heaven, the Father declares Jesus to be His beloved Son.

D. *Created in His Image*

In **verse 27**, we are told that man was created in the image, or likeness of God.

In **John 4:24**, we are told that God is Spirit.

Image refers to God's attributes, His nature. It deals with the fact that we are able to create, have relationships, our morality, have powers of reasoning. Unlike animals, we are self- aware, and have emotions.

We have seen that God is a triune being. We were created as triune beings also.

1. Physical
2. Mind-emotions, will, intellect, thoughts
3. Spirit-part of us that will live eternally-our conscience, our knowledge of right from wrong, our ability to have a relationship with God. We were made for God's glory with the purpose of reflecting His image.

> everyone who is called by My name, whom I created for my glory, whom I formed and made." ***Isaiah 43:7***

> This people I formed for Myself they shall shew forth My praise. ***Isaiah 43:21***

E. *Purpose of Creation*

1. God's creation was designed by God to display the glory of God.

    > The heavens declare the glory of God; and the firmament shows His handiwork. ***Psalm 19:1***

    > A man should not wear anything on his head when worshiping, for man is made in God's image and reflects God's glory. And woman reflects man's glory ***1 Corinthians 11:7***

    > You are worthy O Lord, to receive glory, and honor, and power: for You have created all things, and for Your pleasure they are and were created. ***Revelation 4:11***

2. Another purpose of creation is to reveal God's invisible qualities-His eternal power and divine nature.

> But God shows his anger from heaven against all sinful, wicked people who suppress the truth by their wickedness. 19 They know the truth about God because He has made it obvious to them. 20 For ever since the world was created, people have seen the earth and sky. Through everything God made, they can clearly see his invisible qualities—His eternal power and divine nature. So they have no excuse for not knowing God. ***Romans 1:18-20***

F. *Man's Dominion*

We are told in **verse 28** that man was to have dominion over the earth. We were made to rule with God over His creation. Having dominion involves reigning over, having authority. God is the owner, because He made the world. We are stewards, or caretakers over His creation.

> The highest heavens belong to the LORD, but the earth he has given to man. ***Psalm 115:16***

> You made him a little lower than the heavenly beings and crowned him with glory and honor. 6 You made him ruler over the works of your hands; you put everything under his feet: 7all flocks and herds, and the beasts of the field, 8the birds of the air, and the fish of the sea, all that swim the paths of the seas. ***Psalm 8:5-8***

G. *First Command*

> **Verse 28** gives the first command given by God.

H. *God is a Good God of Blessing*

> God desires to bless us.

> **Verse 22, 28** …Then God blessed them…

I.   *Names of God*

There are many names for God found throughout the Bible. In this chapter He is simply referred to as *God*. This is from the Hebrew word Elohim. It refers to God's power and might.

DAY FIVE

SUMMARY

God's reign is exercised by His Word, His will, and His works. His creating "good things" reveals His benevolence and His holy nature.[5]

God created the universe according to His will, for His own purpose, and by His own power.

Because God created everything, He has the right to rule over everything.

For Further Study

Do a concordance search on the words ***creation, sabbath***
Look at the following
   Job 38
   Psalm 104
   Isaiah 40:25: 42:5.

WEEK TWO
Adam and Eve

Outline

A. Sabbath **vs 1-3**

B. Creation of man **vs 4-7**

C. Planting of Garden of Eden **vs 8-15**

D. First Command given-consequences stated **vs 16-17**

E. Adam names animals but finds no suitable helper **vs 18-20**

F. First surgery-God created woman **vs 21-23**

G. Institution of marriage **vs 23-24**

Day One

Observation- Genesis 2

1. What are we told that the Lord did on the seventh day?

2. What unusual condition existed at this time? see **verses 5-6**

3. How was the creation of man different from the creation of the animals?

4. What special home did God make for man?

5. a. What two specific trees are mentioned in **vs 9**?
   b. Where was one of these trees located?

6. What four rivers flowed out of Eden

7. What was in the land of Havilah?

8. According to **verse 15**, what are two reasons that God put man in the garden?

9. a. What specific instructions did God give to the man?
   b. What warning did God give to Adam?
   c. Why was this command given?

10. Who named the animals?

11. What is the only thing that God says is not good? see **verse 18**.

12. What did God do to correct the one thing that was not good?

13. a. Who instituted marriage?
    b. What are the three elements involved in marriage?

14. What are we told about Adam and Eve in **verse 25**?

15. What do we learn about God from this account?

II. Correlation-Comparing Other Texts

A. *Sabbath*

God wants us to honor the Sabbath by resting from work and focusing on worship.

Under the law it was required that Israel observe the seventh day as a Sabbath of rest.

    1.   What do the following verses tell us about the Sabbath?
Exodus 20:8-11; 31:12-17
Deuteronomy 5:12-14
Isaiah 58:13-14
Hebrews 4:5-11

    2.   a. Who was the Sabbath for? See **Mark 2:27-28**
         b. According to **verse 28,** who is Lord over the Sabbath?

B. *Spirit*
    1.   What does **Proverbs 20:27** say concerning the spirit of a man?

C. *Two Adams*
    1.   Who is the second Adam? How is he different from the first Adam?
See **Romans 5:12-21; 1 Corinthians 15:45.**

D. *Marriage*
    1.   What is God's attitude toward marriage according to **Malachi 2:16**?

    2.   Look at **Matthew 19:4-10**
         a.   What does Jesus say about marriage in **verses 4-6**?
         b.   What did Jesus say was the reason Moses permitted divorce?

    c.   What did Jesus say was the only basis for divorce?
    d.   What did Jesus say of someone who divorced and remarried?
    e.   What was the response of the disciples to this teaching?

3. a. What does Paul say concerning marriage in **1 Corinthians 7:2-5,10-11,27**?
b. What does Paul say concerning marriage to an unbeliever in **1 Corinthians 7:12-13,15**?
c. What is the reason he gives for this instruction in **verse 14,16**?

4. What instructions concerning marriage are we given in the following verses?
Ephesians 5:25-28,33
Colossians 3:18-19
1 Peter 3:1-2,7
Hebrews 13:4

5. What example does Paul use concerning wives in marriage in **1 Peter 3:5-6**?

6. What special exemption was given to a man who had just married in **Deuteronomy 24:5**?

Day Two

COMMENTARY

vs 5-6 When the earth was new, there was no rain. It didn't rain until the great flood. The earth was watered by a mist-like dew.

vs 7 God …breathed into man the breath of life. Man differs from the rest of creation because we have a soul.

The human body is made from elements found in the ground.

vs15 The word *care* in this verse has the idea of serving. The word is translated as *worship* elsewhere. Recall the instruction we are given in ***Romans 12:1***

> Therefore, I urge you, brothers, in view of God's mercy, to offer your bodies as living sacrifices, holy and pleasing to God-this is your spiritual act of worship.

vs 21-23 Here we have the first surgery by the Great Physician

Woman was to be man's helper.

> 8 For the first man didn't come from woman, but the first woman came from man. 9 And man was not made for woman, but woman was made for man. 10 For this reason, and because the angels are watching, a woman should wear a covering on her head to show she is under authority.
>
> 11 But among the Lord's people, women are not independent of men, and men are not independent of women. 12 For although the first woman came from man, every other man was born from a woman, and everything comes from God. ***1 Corinthians 11:8-12***

Digging Deeper-Lessons learned from the passage

A. Why Two Accounts

These two accounts are not contradictory. **Genesis 1** is a broad overall account of the creation. **Genesis 2** is a more specific and detailed account focusing on the creation of man, the crown of creation.

B. *God rested.*

God didn't rest because He was tired. He rested because His work was complete.

C. *The Sabbath*

Verse 2-3 tells us that God rested on the seventh day, blessing it and sanctifying it-making it holy.

This became known as the *Sabbath* and was set aside as a day of rest and worship. The word comes from Hebrew Shavat, meaning to rest.

It is one of the ten commandments that was given to Moses.

It is a time meant to focus on God and His goodness. When we fail to do this our lives get out of balance. We need time with God and His Word to keep our lives from getting off track and out of whack.

> "Remember the Sabbath day by keeping it holy. ^{9}Six days you shall labor and do all your work, ^{10}but the seventh day is a Sabbath to the LORD your God. On it you shall not do any work, neither you, nor your son or daughter, nor your manservant or maidservant, nor your animals, nor the alien within your gates. ^{11}For in six days the LORD made the heavens and the earth, the sea, and all that is in them, but he rested on the seventh day. Therefore the LORD blessed the Sabbath day and made it holy. ***Exodus 20:8***

> "Observe the Sabbath day by keeping it holy, as the LORD your God has commanded you. ^{13}Six days you shall labor and do all your work, ^{14}but the seventh day is a Sabbath to the LORD your God. On it you shall not do any work, neither you, nor your son or daughter, nor your manservant or maidservant, nor your ox, your donkey or any of your animals, nor the alien within your gates,

so that your manservant and maidservant may rest, as you do. 15Remember that you were slaves in Egypt and that the LORD your God brought you out of there with a mighty hand and an outstretched arm. Therefore the LORD your God has commanded you to observe the Sabbath day. ***Deuteronomy 5:12***

"If you keep your feet from breaking the Sabbath and from doing as you please on My holy day, if you call the Sabbath a delight and the Lord's holy day honorable, and if you honor it by not going your own way and not doing as you please or speaking idle words, 14 then you will find your joy in the Lord and I will cause you to ride on the heights of the land and to feast on the inheritance of your father Jacob." The mouth of the Lord has spoken. ***Isaiah 58:13-14***

D. *The Garden of Eden*

Location

Of the four rivers mentioned, only two of them are known today- the Tigris and Euphrates. The area between these two rivers is known as "the fertile crescent", and has also been called the "cradle of civilization".

This is the area where Mesopotamia is located. The word is Greek and means "land between the rivers". It is now part of Iraq.

E. *Man's Responsibilities*

Man is given the task of caring for the garden. This responsibility resulted in:
1. Challenging work:
   a. rule and authority over God's creation **1:28**
   b. fill earth and subdue it. **1:28**

       c.   work and care for garden **2:15**
       d.   name animals **2:19-20**

  2.   Free will to chose to obey God

  3.   Companionship with each other

  4.   Priviledge of fellowship with their Creator

  5.   Be fruitful and multiply

F.   *Clear Warning*

In **verse 17** God gives clear warning concerning the consequences for failure to obey His directive. God is to be obeyed. There are serious consequences for failure to do so. This was a test of obedience. The Lord wanted their willing obedience, not forced obedience. If their obedience was forced, they would not have fellowship, they would be slaves. God wanted a relationship with His creation. In order for there to be a relationship, man had to have free choice of whether or not to obey God.

God did not want man to be burdened with the knowledge of evil. Knowing evil would mean their innocence would be lost.

G.   *Naming*

In **verse 19** the Lord brought the animals to Adam, who then named them. The act of naming something symbolized rulership or authority over what was being named.

H.   *Marriage*

In this passage, we learn that marriage was God's idea. It involves:
    leaving-parents
    cleaving-being joined to lifetime partner

becoming one, unity-in body, mind and spirit. This oneness ultimately results in children.
union between *one man and one woman*
it is meant to be a permanent commitment.

Matthew Henry says that Eve "was not taken from Adam's head to rule over him, or from his foot to be ruled by him, but from next to his heart symbolizing that she was to be loved and cherished and his helper and companion."[6]

I.   Names of God

In this chapter God is referred to as *Lord God*. This is from the Hebrew Yahweh. In the Hebrew there were no vowels in the word because it was revered so highly that the name was never to be spoken. This name refers to all God is, His character, His self-existent nature.

J.   And they were Naked...and Not Ashamed

This shows their state of purity and innocence. To be naked is to be completely exposed and vulnerable.

At this point, Adam and Eve have God's
    Presence
    Provision-of home, food, partner

Word Wealth

Adam is Hebrew for man.

Adamah is Hebrew for ground.

Eden is Hebrew for delight or pleasantness, or pleasure.

The word *formed* (**vs 7**) is a translation of the Hebrew word yatsur. It has the idea of forming something into something else, like a potter forms, or shapes clay.

The Hebrew and Greek words for *spirit*-living being in **verse 7** can also be translated as breath or wind. So when God breathed into man, He was actually breathing His spirit into him. The breath of God gave man spiritual life-soul-self awareness.

rib-Hebrew tsela means side.

SUMMARY

God through the act of creation gives form and fills what had previously been formless and empty. From this account we learn that God is the source and sustainer of all things.

Day Three-

The Rebellion

Observation-Genesis 3

1. a. Who is spoken of in **verse 1**?
   b. What information are we given concerning this creature?
   c. What do the words cunning, subtle, crafty, or shrewd mean?
   d. What does this creature tempt Eve to do?

2. Compare **Genesis 3:1,4** with **Genesis 2:16-17**.

3. Compare **Genesis 3:3** with **Genesis 2:17**.

How does Eve change the command given by the Lord?

4. What does the serpent claim Eve could gain by disobeying the command of the Lord?

5. What was the serpent right about?

6. What do we learn about Satan from this account?

7. What aspects does Eve note about the forbidden fruit?

8. How do Adam and Eve react when they:
   a. realized they were naked
   b. hear the Lord walking in the garden?
   c. are confronted by God?

9. What made them hide from the Lord?

10. a. What questions does the Lord ask in this account?
    b. Who are the questions directed to?

11. What are Adam and Eve's response when confronted with what they had done?

12. What were the judgments given by God to:
    a. the serpent
    b. Eve
    c. Adam

13. Who, or what did the Lord curse?

14. What did Adam name his wife?

15. a. What did the Lord make for Adam and Eve?
    b. What were they made from?

16. How did God show grace to Adam and Eve?

17. What New Testament event does **Genesis 3:15** foreshadow?

18. a. What did the Lord do concerning the garden of Eden?
    b. Why did he do this?

19. What do we learn about the Lord from this account?

20. Mark all the Lord's actions:
    a. He called
    b. God walking
    c. God asked
    d. God said
    e. God made
    f. God cursed
    g. God sent
    h. God drove out
    i. God commanded

21. What lessons can we apply to our lives from this account?

Day Four

Correlation- Comparing Other Texts

A. *Who is the serpent?*

1. What are we told concerning the serpent in the following verses?
   Revelation 12:9
   Revelation 20:2

2. What does Jesus say about the devil in **John 8:44**?

3. What are we told about Satan in **1 John 3:8**?

4. a. What is Satan's desire according to **1 Peter 5:8**?
   b. What do we learn about Satan's desire from **Isaiah 14:13**?

5. What are we told Satan does in **Mark 4:15**?

6. What do we learn about Satan's control in **1 John 5:19**?

7. What do we learn about Satan from **2 Corinthians 11:14**?

8. a. What are we told about what power Satan holds in **Hebrews 2:14**?
   b. What results from fear of death according to **verse 15**?

B. *How Are We to Deal Satan?*

1. What are we told to do in the following verses about dealing with Satan?
   1 Peter 5:9
   James 4:7?

2. What are our weapons against Satan according to **Ephesians 6:11-18**.

3. What instructions are we given concerning how we are to deal with those who are captives of Satan in **2 Timothy 2:25-26**?

C. *Temptation Verses Testing*

1. Is it a sin to be tempted?

WEEK TWO | 35

2. What is the cause of temptation accrding to **James 1:14**?

3. Who is not the cause of temptation according to **James 1:13**?

4. What are the stages of temptation found in **James 1:14-15**?

5. What does submitting to sin result in according to **James 1:15**?

6. What instruction does Jesus give for combating temptation in **Matthew 26:41**?

7. What warning do we find in **1 Corinthians 10:12?**

8. What promise concerning temptation do we find in **1 Corinthians 10:13?**

D. *Adam and Eve's Choice*

1. What are we told about Adam's role in the fall according to **1 Timothy 2:14**?

2. What is Paul's concern in **2 Corinthians 11:3**?

3. What are we told about rebellion in **1 Samuel 15:23**?

4. What was the result of Adam chosing to eat the forbidden fruit according to the following verses?
Romans 5:12, 14, 17-19
1 Corinthians 15:22?

5. What else was affected by Adam and Eve's choice according to **Romans 8:20-22**?

6. What does **2 Peter 1:4** tell us causes the corruption of the world?

E. *Impact of the Fall*

Through their disobedience to God and submitting to the temptation of Satan, man forfeited his rule to Satan.

1. What does Jesus call Satan in **John 12:31; 14:30**?

2. What did Adam and Eve's action result in according to **Romans 5:12**?

3. What else was affected by Adam and Eve's choice according to **Romans 8:20-21**?

F. *Fixing the Problem*

1. How do Adam and Eve attempt to fix the problem?

2. What are we told is required in **Hebrews 9:22**?

3. What does **2 Corinthians 5:18** say Jesus did?

4. How can we escape from the corruption in the world according to **2 Peter 1:3-4**?

5. Adam and Eve tried to hide from God out of fear and shame. We often react the same way. What do the following verse tell us about how we should deal with sin?
Proverbs 28:13
1 John 1:9

6. What can we do so we don't sin according to **Psalm 119:11**?

G. *The Promise*

   1. What does **Revelation 13:8** tell us about the promise God made in **Genesis 3:15**?

   2. What does **1 John 3:8** say was the reason the Son of God appeared?

   3. What does **1 Corinthians 15:26** say is the last enemy?
   4. a Who is the fulfillment of the promise according to **1 Corinthians 15:22, 45-49**?
      b. How does the second Adam differ from the first?

H. *Jesus is the Answer*

   1. a. What are we learn about Jesus in **Hebrews 2:14-18; 4:15; 5:15-17**?
      b. What does this experience enable Him to do for us?

I. *Cherubim*

Cherubims were winged creatures. They are described in a vision seen by Ezekiel-see **Ezekiel 1:5-24; 10:8-17, 21; 41:18-19**.

Replicas of Cherubim were found on the mercy seat of the ark of the covenant-see **Exodus 25:18-22**.

Apparently they are guardians of the Lord's presence.

J. *The Tree of Life*

   1. Where is the tree of life now located according to **Revelation 22:1-2**?

   2. a. What does the tree of life bear according to **Revelation 22:2**?

b. What are its leaves used for?

3. Who will be permitted to eat of the fruit from the tree according to **Revelation 22:14**?

4. Who will not be able to eat from the tree according to **Revelation 22:19**?

Word Wealth

Eve - living or life

Satan - means adversary

Devil - Greek diabolos-means accuser or slanderer

Enmity - strife, hostility against another

Curse - to call evil or injury down on; to bring evil or injury on; afflict

tempt - to try, test, or prove, to try to persuade; induce or entice.

sin - Greek hamartia-missing the mark, failure, offense, taking the wrong course, wrongdoing, guilt.[7]

Commentary

vs 1 This is the first question in Scripture.

Satan was a created being, an angelic being who rebelled against God and was thrown out of heaven. See **Isaiah 14:12-15; Ezekiel 28:12-15.**

We don't know how long after God created the angels that Satan rebelled. We also don't know how long after God created Adam and Eve that Eve was tempted by Satan.

vs 2-3 Notice Eve's focus. She isn't focused on the abundance of God's provision, but on the one prohibition. She focuses on where it is, not the fact that it is a danger-eating of it will cause them to "surely die". Even the serpent uses these words.

vs 6 Eve's choice was self serving and was not concerned with honoring or glorifying her Creator. It was an act of rebellion and an attempt to become her own god.

vs 8 Imagine the privilege of God walking with them. Yet now they hide from Him in fear.

vs 10 This is the first we find the word fear in the Bible.

vs 11 God is giving Adam a chance to confess his sin. This is what we all must do.

We are promised in **1 John 1:9** If we confess our sins, he is faithful and just to forgive us our sins, and to cleanse us from all unrighteousness.

vs 14 Here we find the first use of the word *curse* in the Bible.

vs 15 This is the first promise of a Savior. We can't save ourselves.

vs 17 Man's labor now would result in sorrow and frustration instead of joy and fulfillment.

vs 22 Notice again the reference to "us". God did not want man to live forever in His fallen state.

What is meant by "the fall"? It does not mean that Adam and Eve "fell" into sin. It refers to the fact that they made a choice. And because of that choice they lost "dominion" over God's creation. By disobeying God, man forfeited his role to the serpent. Jesus referred to Satan as the "prince of this world" in **John 12:31**. He calles him the "ruler of the world" in **John 14:30** and **John 16:11**.

Day Five Digging Deeper-Lessons to be Learned

A. *Beware of Satan's Tactics*

Satan causes Eve to question God's:
    motives-His goodness
    trustworthiness
    command-authority

He gets her to reset her focus from what she had to covet what she doesn't have, shouldn't have and doesn't need.

His tactics haven't changed. His seduction is-Why worship God when you could be a god yourself?

Satan then calls God a liar-and challenges God's authority. Satan's goal is to become God-overthrow God's authority.

Satan is a great deceiver. He works by telling half truths. He successfully tempted Eve by getting her to doubt God's goodness. He made her forget all that God had given her and done for her, getting her to focus on the one thing that God denied her to have. He is still working the same way today. We need to develop an attitude of gratitude, and be content with what we have. Many of the ten commandments warn us against coveting. We need to focus on the many blessings God has given us-not on the blessings He has given others. When we get greedy and want more, we become discontent and unappreciative of what we do have. Adam and Eve had everything they needed, but weren't satisfied. They wanted more and lost everything.

Satan claimed that Adam and Eve could be as wise as God, but that God wanted to reserve this knowledge for Himself. Satan was claiming that they could know the difference between good and evil by doing evil. Evil is going against the will of God. We sometimes believe that freedom is being able to do anything we want to. God says that freedom is obeying what He tells us, and knowing what not to do.

Satan claims that we can become like God by defying His authority, and by becoming our own god. He claims that we don't need God, and that doing what we want even though we know it is wrong makes us like God. What a contradiction! God is holy and just. He only does what is right.

To become like God is humanity's highest goal. To become LIKE God is not to become God Himself, but to reflect His characteristics and recognize His authority over our life.

The goal of self-exaltation is rebellion against God, and rebellion against God is a sin.

Satan's goal is to confuse and mislead us. That is one reason it is so important for us to know the Lord's Word for ourselves. Satan knows the Bible-See Jesus' temptation **Luke 4:1-12**. But he twists God's Word and if we don't know the Word, we will be deceived.

B. *Temptation Verses Testing*

It is not a sin to be tempted-Jesus Himself was tempted by Satan. It becomes sin when we submit to the temptation.

God is never the source of temptation. He does test people to see if they will obey Him, as he did with the Tree of Knowledge and with Abraham when He instructed him to sacrifice his son Isaac. The purpose of testing is to show our love for God. Temptation always leads us to disobey God.

God desires our obedience.

Whoever has My commands and obeys them, he is the one who loves Me. He who loves Me will be loved by my Father, and I too will love him and show Myself to him."
John 14:21

But if anyone obeys His word, God's love is truly made complete in him. This is how we know we are in Him: 6Whoever claims to live in Him must walk as Jesus did.
1 John 2:5

In **Micah 6:8** we are told that the Lord desires us to:
    act justly
    love mercy
    walk humbly with God-to walk in obedience to Him

God wants us to obey Him, but He gives us free-will. He doesn't force our obedience. He is not a dictator who demand s our obedience. He desires us to obey Him out of our love for HIm.

C.   *Steps Into Sin*

Look at **Verse 6**. Eve took three steps that led her to sin.
    1.   She contemplated-considered
    2.   She rationalized
    3.   She consented

John speaks of this in **1 John 2:16** For everything in the world--the cravings of sinful man, the lust of his eyes and the boasting of what he has and does--comes not from the Father but from the world. We see these same steps taken by two other people recorded in the Bible.

In **Joshua 7** after the great victory at Jericho, the people are defeated by a smaller town called Ai. Joshua is told that it is because "Israel has sinned"-**vs 11**. It is then found out that a man named Achan had taken some items from the plunder of Jericho, which had been forbidden. Notice his confession in **verse 21**:

> When *I saw* in the plunder a beautiful robe from Babylonia, two hundred shekels of silver and a wedge of gold weighing fifty shekels, *I coveted* them and *took them.* They are hidden in the ground inside my tent, with the silver underneath."

He saw, coveted, and took.

We see in **2 Samuel 11:2,4** that David saw Bathsheba, coveted her and took her.

The root of all sin is independence from God. It is rebellion against God and lack of faith in God's goodness and sovereignty.

Disobedience is doing things our way-not God's way. Eve chose her way instead of God's way. She wasn't concerned about glorifying God.

As we are told in **James 4:7**, we need to resist the devil, not socialize with him.

This incident shows that a person's circumstances are not what causes them to sin. Adam and Eve had everything but they weren't satisfied- they wanted more.

> but each one is tempted when, by his own evil desire, he is dragged away and enticed. [15]Then, after desire has conceived, it gives birth to sin; and sin, when it is full-grown, gives birth to death. ***James 1:14-15***

Here we learn that it is our own evil desires that tempt us.

In the King James version it says "he is drawn away of his own lust". *enticed-*to seduce, persuade, lure with bait.

*lust-*a desire to gratify the senses; bodily appetite; an intense over-mastering desire.

Lust is a matter of the heart.

> "You have heard that it was said, `Do not commit adultery.' ²⁸But I tell you that anyone who looks at a woman lustfully has already committed adultery with her in his heart. ***Matthew 5:27-28***

How can we combat lust according to **Galatians 5:16**?

D. *How to Effectively Deal with Temptation*

Remember, we all face temptation.
> No temptation has seized you except what is common to man. **1 Corinthians 10:13a**

1. Run!

This is what Joseph did when he was confronted with Pontiphar's wife.

> Now Joseph was well-built and handsome, ⁷and after a while his master's wife took notice of Joseph and said, "Come to bed with me!"
>
> ⁸But he refused ⁹No one is greater in this house than I am. My master has withheld nothing from me except you, because you are his wife. How then could I do such a wicked thing and sin against God?" ¹⁰And though she spoke to Joseph day after day, he refused to go to bed with her or even be with her.
>
> ¹¹One day he went into the house to attend to his duties, and none of the household servants was inside. 12She caught him by his cloak and said, "Come to bed with me!" But he left his cloak in her hand and *ran out of the house.* **Genesis 39:6-12**

2. Pray for strength to resist.

> And lead us not into temptation,

but deliver us from the evil one. ***Matthew 6:13***

"Watch and pray so that you will not fall into temptation. The spirit is willing, but the body is weak." ***Matthew 26:41***

3. Be on guard.

   But watch yourself, or you also may be tempted. ***Galatians 6:1b***

   Be self-controlled and alert. Your enemy the devil prowls around like a roaring lion looking for someone to devour. 9Resist him, standing firm in the faith... ***1 Peter 5:8-9***

4. Submit to God, resist the devil.

   Submit yourselves, then, to God. Resist the devil, and he will flee from you. ***James 4:7***

E. *Their Eyes Were Opened*

What were they opened to? What knowledge had they gained? Well now they knew sin, evil, shame and eventually death, and their relationship with the Lord is now marred.

Sin results in shame. Webster's dictionary defines shame as a painful emotion caused by consciousness of guilt, shortcoming, or impropriety in one's behavior or position.

F. *Where Are You*

God didn't ask this because He didn't know where they were. The question pointed out their lost state.

G. *Blame Game*

When God confronts Adam, Adam's response was to blame Eve, and even imply that God might be somewhat to blame making the statement "The woman *you* put here with me". Eve then blamed the serpent who of course didn't have a leg to stand on.

Often people blame others or circumstances for their personal failures. God knows the truth and will hold us responsible for what we do.

H. *Consequences*

Sin always results in consequences. Sin causes us to experience fear and shame. It robs us of peace of mind and emotions. Loss of peace is a symptom of being outside of God's will.
The consequences of their actions resulted in:

    a.   separation from
               God
               each other
    b.   loss of harmony
    c.   Guilt
    d.   blame
    e.   shame
    f.   fear
    g.   realize they were naked-loss of innocence
    h.   banishment from their home
    i.   tyranny to headship
    j.   rebellion to submission

It often causes consequences for innocent people as well as those guilty of the sin. If someone chooses to drive drunk and kills someone, commit murder, steal, etc., an innocent person suffers due to another person's evil actions.

In this case, an innocent animal had to die to provide covering for Adam and Eve, as well as the ground being cursed.

God had told Adam he would die the day he ate of the forbidden fruit. He didn't die physically immediately, but started the process of dying from that moment. He did however die spiritually. His relationship with God was broken.

Adam's sin did result in the first death-that of an innocent animal.

I. Fixing the Problem

Adam and Eve try to cover themselves by sewing together fig leaves. They could not fix their situation themselves. Sinners are unable to cover their sin on their own. They were guilty and their just punishment was death. But God showed mercy and took an animal as a substitute. We are told in **Hebrews 9:22** that shed blood is required for cleansing and forgiveness.

Their sin resulted in the break down of our fellowship with God. God sent His son Jesus Christ, to open the way for us to renew our fellowship with Him. Our response is fear, because we know that we are unworthy.

God gave both Adam and Eve the chance to confess and repent, through asking them questions. Notice He does not ask the serpent any questions. He does not give the serpent any opportunity to confess and repent. He curses the serpent-see **verse 14.**

God also showed mercy by not letting Adam and Eve live in an eternal state of sin. This was the reason He banned them from access to the tree of life.

J.   The Promise

In **verse 15**, God makes a promise of a Savior. The rest of the Bible documents the fulfillment of this promise.
Jesus is God's fulfillment of His promise.

> "For God so loved the world that he gave His one and only Son,F that whoever believes in Him shall not perish but have eternal life. [17]For God did not send His Son into the world to condemn the world, but to save the world through Him. 18Whoever believes in Him is not condemned, but whoever does not believe stands condemned already because he has not believed in the name of God's one and only Son. *John 3:16-18*

> For as in Adam all die, so in Christ all will be made alive. *1 Corinthians 15: 22*

> Therefore, just as sin entered the world through one man, and death through sin, and in this way death came to all men, because all sinned.

> [17]For if, by the trespass of the one man, death reigned through that one man, how much more will those who receive God's abundant provision of grace and of the gift of righteousness reign in life through the one man, Jesus Christ. *Romans 5:12,17*

Jesus has again given us open access to God.

> Therefore, brothers, since we have confidence to enter the Most Holy Place by the blood of Jesus, [20]by a new and living way opened for us through the curtain, that is, his body, *Hebrews 10:19-20*

Jesus is the only way to gain access to the Lord.

> Jesus answered, "I am the way and the truth and the life. No one comes to the Father except through me. *John 14:6*

2 Corinthians 5:18-19 tells us that Jesus has reconciled us to God.

> ¹⁸And all of this is a gift from God, who brought us back to himself through Christ. And God has given us this task of reconciling people to him. 19 For God was in Christ, reconciling the world to himself, no longer counting people's sins against them. And he gave us this wonderful message of reconciliation.

SUMMARY

In this account we learn that God does judge sin, but He is also a merciful, forgiving and loving God.
In **Exodus 34:6** the Lord states of Himself,

> "The LORD, the LORD, the compassionate and gracious God, slow to anger, abounding in love and faithfulness, 7maintaining love to thousands, and forgiving wickedness, rebellion and sin. Yet He does not leave the guilty unpunished.

We see here the beginnings of His plan of salvation.

God is seeking the lost, calling to them "Where are you?" Are you hiding from God? If you are, He is calling to you and desires for you to repent and return to Him.

That was the purpose for which Jesus came.

> For the Son of man is come to seek and to save that which was lost. *Luke 19:10*

By giving in to Satan's temptation to disobey the Lord, Adam and Eve gave their dominion of the earth over to Satan. When Satan tempted Jesus, He showed Jesus all the kingdoms of the world and said, "I will give you their splendor and all this authority, because it has been given over to me, and I can give it to anyone I want." **Luke 4:6** Jesus didn't state otherwise.

We need to have an attitude of gratitude. Satan wants us to focus on what we don't have instead of being grateful for the provision of God. God provides for all of our needs. He doesn't necessarily provide all of our wants.

The whole rest of the Bible is the story of God through history seeking the lost culminating in His sending His own Son with the mission to "seek and save the lost" *Luke 19:10.*

Eve was named by Adam "because she was the mother of all the living" **vs 20** She was also the reason they all would die.

Every one of us is tempted.

> There hath no temptation taken you but such as is common to man: but God is faithful, who will not suffer you to be tempted above that ye are able; but will with the temptation also make a way to escape, that ye may be able to bear it. *1 Corinthians 10:13*

APPLICATON

We were given free choice by God. Are you making wise decisions? Would God approve of your choices? Are you taking responsibility for your decisions?

Are you hiding from God?

Is there an area in your life where you are being tempted? Lying, stealing, adultery, pornography, substance abuse? What will you do about it?

Has Satan fed you the lie that your sin is unforgivable? Has guilt made you feel unworthy to relate to God?

Don't fall for Satan's lie. Remember that God loves you and is merciful. All you have to do is ask for His forgiveness and accept the work that His Son did on your behalf to pay the price of your sin.

The Deception of the Serpent in Genesis 3

Promises made by Satan	Perceptions of Adam and Eve	Results
Not die	Good for food	Eyes opened to nakedness and shame
be like God	Pleasant to the eyes	hid from God
know good and evil	Desirable to make one wise	blamed one another -relationship with each other affected

Who Did What

vs	What God Did	What Satan Did	What Man Did
2:7	Formed man		
2:8a	Planted garden		
2:8b,15	Put man in garden		cultivated garden
2:16-17	Commanded man not to eat from tree		obeyed God
2:19a	formed beasts and birds		
2:19b,20	Brought animals to man		named animals

2:21-24	Made woman		man and woman cleaved to each other
3:1-5		tempted woman lied	
3:6			ate forbidden fruit
3:7			Made coverings
3:8-9	Called to Adam		Hid from God
3:11,13	Questioned Adam and Eve		Placed blame
3:14	Cursed serpent		
3:16 -1-19	Judged Adam and Eve		
3:20			Named Eve

WEEK THREE
Mankind's Downward Spiral

Day One

Observation- Genesis 4

1.   a. Who were Adam and Eve's firstborn?
   b. What does the name mean?
   c. What was his occupation?

2.   a. What was the name of Adam and Eve's second son?
   b. What does the name mean?
   c. What was his occupation?

3.   a. What did Cain and Abel do in **vs 3-4**?
   b. Compare the offerings given. What are the differences?
   c. What does this indicate about the ones making the sacrifices?

4.   a. How does the Lord respond toward the sacrifices?
   b. How did Cain react to the Lord's response?

5. What warning did God give to Cain?

6.   a. What did Cain do?
   b. What was his motive for doing this?

7.   a. What does the Lord ask Cain?

    b. How is God's dealing with Cain here similar to His dealing earlier with Adam?

8. a. What was the punishment given to Cain by God?
    b. One part of Cain's punishment was that he was driven from the ground. Why was this given as part of his punishment?
    c. What was Cain's response to his punishment?

9. a. What did Cain fear would happen?
    b. What did God do to prevent this from happening?

10. How did God show mercy to Cain?

11. What do we learn about God from this incident?

12. Where did Cain go to live?

13. Who was Cain's son?

14. a. What did Cain build?
    b. Who did he name it after?

15. a. What are we told about Lamech in **verse 19**?
    b. What were their names?

16. a. What were the names of Adah's sons?
    b. What were their occupations?

17. a. What were the names of Zillah's son's?
    b. What were their occupations?

18. a. What did Lamech do?
    b. Why did he do this?

19. a. Who was the third son of Adam and Eve?
    b. What does his name mean?

20. Who was Adam and Eve's grandson?

21. What did men begin to do when Seth's son was born?

Day Two

Correlation- Comparing other Texts

1. What do we learn about Cain and Abel's sacrifices in **Hebrews 11:4?**

2. a. What do we learn about this incident in **1 John 3:10-12?**
   b. According to these verses, what was Cain's motive?

A. Sin
   1. How does the Bible define sin? See the following texts:
      1 John 3:4
      Romans 14:23b
      James 4:17
      Isaiah 53:6a

   2. Sin means to miss the mark. What mark have we missed according to **Romans 3:23?**

   3. According to the following verses, who is guilty of sin?
      Kings 8:46
      Chronicles 6:36
      Ecclesiastes 7:20
      1 John 1:8,10
      Romans 3:23
      Romans 5:12

4. How does **Isaiah 53:6a** describe our condition?

5. What are the wages we receive for sin according to **Romans 6:23**?

6. What do we learn from **Ephesians 2:1-2** about:
   a. result of sin
   b. Who we belong to when we sin?

7. What warning about sin do we find in **Numbers 32:23**?

8. What is the effect of sin according to **John 8:34; Romans 6:16,20**?

9. How are we freed from sin according to **Romans 6:6-7,11**?

10. What instructions about sin are we given in **Romans 6:12-13**?

11. What are we not to let sin do according to **Romans 6:14**?

12. a. What does **Hebrews 12:1** tell us about sin?
    b. What does this verse instruct us to do with sin?

13. a. What are we told about those who keep sinning in **1 John 3:6,9**?
    b. Who do those who keep on sinning belong to according to **1 John 3:8**?

14. a. What are we told about the sinful nature in **2 Peter 2:10**?
    b. What does this nature despise?

15. How can we combat the desires of the sinful nature according to **Galatians 5:16**?

16. What are we warned against in **Hebrews 3:13**?
17. a. What is our responsibility for others caught in sin according to **Galatians 6:1**?
    b. What warning are we given here?

B. Our Brothers

1. a. What are we told in **1 John 3:15** about anyone who hates their brother?
   b. Who do those who do not love their brother belong to according to **1 John 3:10**?

2. What instruction are we given in **Leviticus 19:17-18** about our brother?
3. What does Jesus say about being angry with our brother in **Matthew 5:21-24**?
4. What are we told in **Galatians 4:14?**

C. God Knows the Heart

1. What do we learn from the following verses?
   1 Kings 8:39
   1 Chronicles 28:9
   Psalm 7:9
   Psalm 139:3-4
   Jeremiah 11:20
   Jeremiah 17:10
   Jeremiah 20:12
   Luke 16:15
   Revelation 2:23

D. Heeding God

1. In **verse 7,** God gives Cain a warning, but Cain ignores it. What does **Hebrews 3:7- 8,15** tell us about not listening to God?

2. What does **Proverbs 3:11-12** instruct us concerning the Lords discipline?

3. What does **Job 5:17** tell us concerning those the Lord corrects? See also **Psalm 94:12**.

4. a. What does the Lord say He does to those He loves in **Revelation 3:19**?
   b. What does He say about how we should respond?

5. What instruction is given in **Hebrews 12:5-6** regarding the Lord's discipline?

E. Cain's Actions

1. What are we told in **1 John 3:12** about Cain and his motive for killing his brother?

F. Sacrifices

1. What instructions are we given in the following verses concerning the sacrifice we are to offer?
   Romans 6:13,19
   Romans 12:1

G. Anger

1. Is being angry a sin? See **Psalm 4:4; Ephesians 4:26**

2. What warning about anger do we find in **Ephesians 4:26-27**?

3. What are we told about anger in **Provebs 20:11**?

4. What instructions does **Psalm 37:8** give concerning anger?

5. What warning about anger are we given in **Ecclesiastes 7:9**?

6. What instructions are we given in the following verses concerning anger?
   Ephesians 4:31-32
   Colossians 3:8

7. What are we told in **James 2:20** that anger does not produce?

H. Hatred

1. What are we told in **1 John 3:15** about a person who hated his brother?

2. What are we instructed to do in **1 John 3:11**?

Day Three

Lessons to be Learned

Outline of the Chapter

I. Cain and Abel
   A. Birth-**vs 1-2**
   B. Occupations-**vs 2**
   C. Sacrifices offered-**vs 3-4**
   D. Warning given- **vs 7**
   E. Murder committed-**vs 8**
   F. Confronted **vs 9-10**
   G. Judgment passed-**vs 11-12**
   H. Response to Judgment **vs 13-14**
   I. Mercy shown-**vs 15**
   J. Wanderings-**vs 16**
   K. Descendants-**vs 17-18**

II. Lamech
   A. Marries-**vs 19**
   B. Children-**vs 20-23**
   C. Murder again-**vs 23-24**

III. Seth

Word Wealth

Cain-name from Hebrew Qayin-from Qanah-two possible meanings: to acquire, or create, or brought forth.

Abel- means breath, trifle or vapor, or temporary.

sin-to miss the mark

Enoch-means dedication, commencement, initiation, or consecrated.

Lamech-means powerful

Naamah-name means lovely or pleasant Adah-means adorned or ornament

Zillah-means shady or tinkling

Jabel-means stream

Jubal-means music

Seth-means granted

Enosh-means weak or frail.

killed-Hebrew-harag-means to slaughter

countenance-face

In this chapter the words anger, murder and sin are found for the first time.

Key words of this chapter are anger, blood, offering, sin and kill.

4:7 master-gain control over. Sin starts in the heart with a small act of disobedience and continues to grow until a person becomes a slave of sin. Sin destroys a person like cancer. Jesus warned us that whoever commits sin is enslaved.

> "Truely, truely I say unto you, whoever commits sin is the servant of sin." ***John 8:34***

    A.   Sacrifices

The Bible gives various reasons why offerings were made. Some reasons were for acknowledgement of sin, thanksgiving for the Lord's provision, or giving honor and glory to the Lord. We aren't told the reason for the sacrifices Cain and Able made, but since the offerings made had to do with their occupation, they might have been a firstfruits offering to thank the Lord for His provision.

Why did God reject Cain's sacrifice? We aren't given the specific reason in the text, but there are two probable reasons:

1. He didn't offer a proper sacrifice
2. He had a wrong motive for giving the sacrifice.

God may have required a blood sacrifice. We are told in **Hebrews 9:22**, the law requires that nearly everything be cleansed with blood, and without the shedding of blood there is no forgiveness.

Notice that Abel did not bring the best or the first fruits. He only brought "some". Able brought "the firstlings of his flock and the fat thereof". He gave the best to God. God does not work on the principle that something is better than nothing. He wants and deserves only the best. He evaluates what we offer Him.

God requres sacrifice. He requires it to be offered the way He prescribes, not any way we chose. He also requires a right attitude.

Cain expected his offering to be accepted simply because it was given, not because of the reason or motive behind its being given. With God it is all about the heart attitude. He isn't interested in ritual.

Here we learn that we cannot enter God's presence on our terms.

    B.   Warning

In **verse** 7 God gives Cain a chance to do what is right- what was expected, proper, and acceptable. He gives Cain a word of correction and a chance to correct his errant way.

He is told to master sin-gain control over it, not be sin's companion.

"sin is crouching"-ready to pounce. These are words we would do well to heed.

From this we learn that the Lord still communicated with man.

    C.   Cain's Response to the Lord's warning

Cain responds wrongly to God's correction. God called for him to repent-to change his way, and to do what was right. Instead Cain rebelled. He becomes angry that his offering was rejected.

Cain's desire to have his own way resulted in stubbornness which then resulted in anger when his way was rejected. Instead of repenting he let his anger turn into rage which resulted in his murdering his brother. How often are we seeing this today. The Columbine shootings are just one example.

Our responses reflect our attitude.

Why did Cain take his anger out on Abel? He was angry with his brother because Abel had made him look bad by offering a better sacrifice.

His actions may also have been meant to mock God-You want a blood sacrifice-take this one.

Here we see the results of not heeding God's warning. God has given us all a conscience which lets us know when we are thinking or doing wrong. The more we ignore it the easier it becomes to do what is wrong.

   D.   Anger

Jealousy leads to resentment which results in anger which if left unchecked grows into hatred and rage which can then end up leading to murder. We are warned against holding anger because it festers and grows. This is why we are told in **Ephesians 4:26** not to let the sun go down on our anger.

We are warned in Proverbs about the dangers of anger.

> Anger is cruel and fury overwhelming,
>
> but who can stand before jealousy? **Proverbs 27:4**

Anger is like a raging fire and is deadly when allowed to get out of control.

We see this progression also in Esau when his brother Jacob had cheated him out of his blessing, as well as in Joseph's brother's.

> Esau held a grudge against Jacob because of the blessing his father had given him. He said to himself, "The days of mourning for my father are near; then I will kill my brother Jacob." ***Genesis 27:41***

> Jacob loved Joseph more than any of his other children because Joseph had been born to him in his old age. So one day Jacob had a special gift made for Joseph—a beautiful robe. 4 But his brothers hated Joseph because their father loved him more than the rest of them. They couldn't say a kind word to him. When Joseph's brothers saw him coming, they recognized him in the distance. As he approached, they made plans to kill him. 19 "Here comes the dreamer!" they said. 20 "Come on, let's kill him and throw him into one of these cisterns. We can tell our father, 'A wild animal has eaten him.' Then we'll see what becomes of his dreams!" **Genesis 37:3-4, 18-20**

Just as Cain hated his righteous brother, the world also hates the righteous.

> Do not be surprised brothers, if the world hates you. **1 John 3:13**

E. Sin

As we learned yesterday, everyone sins.

Sin dwells in all of our hearts. You don't believe this? Does a child have to be taught to lie?

What instruction are we given in this chapter about how we are to deal with sin?

This incident reveals how totally corrupt humans had become. Sin is like a cancer-sin breeds sin. Cain's parents had sinned and now their son had committed an even greater sin.

Perhaps Cain thought that God wouldn't see what he had done. There is no such thing as "private sin". God sees everything.

> The eyes of the Lord are in every place, beholding the evil and the good. ***Proverbs 15:3***

> "Do not be deceived: God cannot be mocked. A man reaps what he sows. 8The one who sows to please his sinful nature, from that nature will reap destruction; the one who sows to please the Spirit, from the Spirit will reap eternal life. ***Galatians 6:7-8***

We reap what we sow. Sin does not only affect the sinner, but causes harm to innocent people as well. We need to always consider the consequences of our actions. Todays society is one of selfishness-with an instant gratification mentality and a motto of "if it feels good do it" with no concern about the consequences or the affects on others. This is why we have an epidemic of divorce in our society. Instead of being concerned about our spouses, the focus is only on self-meeting our own personal wants and desires. If the spouse fails to meet my needs, then just turn them in for a new model.

Here Adam and Eve lose both of their sons.

Sin results in the separation from God's presence. Until we repent of our sins, we cannot be in His presence. But we are promised that if we confess our sins, God will forgive us and cleanse us.

> But if we confess our sins to him, he is faithful and just to forgive us our sins and to cleanse us from all wickedness. ***1 John 1:9***

    F.   Punishment and Judgment

Cain responds to his sin with contempt and a lack of remorse. He is basically saying "What do I care?" He is not concerned with doing what is right. He is only concerned with himself.

Jude 11 speaks of "the way of Cain". This refers to the way of selfishness, hatred and murder.

We are told in **Proverbs 6:16-17** that the Lord "hates" and "detests... hands that kill the innocent."

Cain's judgment was alienation-from his family, from his home, from his occupation and even from the Lord Himself.

We can either accept God's mercy, or receive His judgment.

    G.   Cain's response to The Lord's Judgment

Cain says his punishment is more than he can bear, and is concerned that someone will kill him! He didn't care when he killed his brother! He shows no remorse for what he has done. His only concern was about himself and his punishment. He feels his punishment was "more than he could bear". What audacity! How could he even think about complaining about his punishment even though the Lord had mercifully spared him the death penalty.

The punishment throughout other Scriptures for committing murder is a death sentence.- See **Genesis 9:6 Exodus 21:12; Leviticus 24:17; Numbers 35:16-17.**

Once again the ground is cursed.

    H.   God's Mercy

Here we again see that God is merciful. He doesn't kill Cain which is the punishment he deserved.

    I.   Cain's Descendants

We aren't told the name of Cain's wife. Cain had a son named Enoch.

We are told that Cain built a city and named it after his son.

Cain's descendants are given in **verse 18**.

Application

How often have we received God's grace? If the Lord counted our sins, who could stand?

Day Four

I. *Lamech*

Match the following:

1. Lemach   a. daughter of Lamech
2. Adah and Zillah   b. father of ironworkers
3. Jabel   c. wives of Lamech
4. Jubel   d. married two women
5. Tubal-Cain   e. father of nomads
6. Naamah   f. father of harp and flute musicians

    1. What are we warned not to do in **Proverbs 24:29**?
    2. What are we instructed to not do in **Romans 12:17,19**?

A. Lessons to be learned

    1. Polygamy-vs monogamy

This is the first recorded case of polygamy.

    2. Another Murder-Vengeance

In **verse 23-24** we are told of another murder committed by Cain's descendant. Lamech brags to his wives that he "killed a man for wounding me."

We aren't given the details of how Lamech was wounded, how badly he was wounded, or the name of the man who wounded him.

This was the reason the law "an eye for an eye" was given-to curb revenge.

We are told that "vengeance is mine says the lord, I will repay." See **Levitcus 19:18; Deuteronomy 32:35;**

There is no mention of the Lord or the things of the Lord in the account of Cain and his descendants. The focus is on man's ability without God. It is a worldly, secular society independent of God.

II. *Seth*

1. "At that time men began to call on the name of the LORD."

call upon-to cry out or call aloud. Seth's line was a line that depended upon the Lord, unlike the proud self reliance of the line of Cain's descendants.

SUMMARY

We can either accept God's mercy or His judgment. We cannot enter into God's presence on our own terms.

Make your prayer **Psalm 19:13; Psalm 26:2; Psalm 51:2; Psalm 119:33.**

Abel	*Cain*
shepherd	Farmer
worshipper	wicked
righteous	wanderer
martyr	city builder

Day Five

Descendants of Seth

A. **Looking at the text-Genesis 5**

1. Compare in whose image God created man-in **verse 1** with what we are told about Adam's son in **verse 3**.

2. How old was Adam when Seth was born?

3. a. What phrase is repeated for each person?
   b. What is the exception?

4. Who is the oldest person listed here?

5. How do the two genealogies given here-that of Adam's sons Cain and Seth, differ?

6. Compare the seventh descendant in each genealogy.

7. Compare the two Enochs.

8. Compare the two Lamechs.

9. What was said about Noah when he was born?

10. Who were Noah's sons?

B. **Correlation-Comparing Other Texts**

1. What are we told about Enoch in **Hebrews 11:5**?

2. What does **Jude 14** tell us about Enoch?

3. Who else in the Bible had a similar experience? see **2 Kings 2:11**.

C. Word Wealth

Enosh-means humanity[8]
Enoch-means dedication[9]
Noah-means comfort

D. Commentary

This chapter gives an account of the descendants of Adam through the line of Seth. It was through this line that our Savior Jesus Christ would come.

Each reference to a patriarch gives four details:

1. Name of the patriarch
2. Age of the patriarch at the birth of the son of the blessed line
3. Length of his remaining life after birth of blessed line son
4. Age at which he died

vs 3 God had made man in His image. Now notice here that Seth was in the image of *Adam*. Because Adam and Eve had sinned, any of their offspring would now reflect their image and not the perfect image of God, because they are no longer in a state of innocence and purity, but a fallen state of sin.

and then he died...-Hebrew *muth*

Note that the genealogy of Cain does not give any ages.

vs 21-24 The name Enoch means dedicated. He was dedicated to the Lord.

vs 22 *walked with God*...refers to fellowship and obedience which results in divine blessing. It is a close communion with God. Of all mankind, only Enoch and Elijah (**2 Kings 2:11**) have alone escaped physical death. This speaks of the "blessed hope" of all Christians at the time of the rapture, which the New Testament writers refer to.

> while we look forward with hope to that wonderful day when the glory of our great God and Savior, Jesus Christ, will be revealed. ***Titus 2:13***

> All praise to God, the Father of our Lord Jesus Christ. It is by his great mercy that we have been born again, because God raised Jesus Christ from the dead. Now we live with great expectation, 4 and we have a priceless inheritance—an inheritance that is kept in heaven for you, pure and undefiled, beyond the reach of change and decay. 5 And through your faith, God is protecting you by his power until you receive this salvation, which is ready to be revealed on the last day for all to see. ***1 Peter 1:3-5***

vs 27 Methuselah is the oldest man recorded in the Bible. His name means "when he is gone it will come". What would come would be the Flood.

There is mention of Cain's descendants being associated in Adam's written genealogy. See Gen 5:1

Cain's descendants continue to demonstrate violence, while Seth's descendants call upon and worship the Lord.

The two Lamech's in each genealogy make use of the number seven, which is the number of completeness and perfection. God rested on the seventh day, because His work was complete.

Cain's Lamech refers to the sevenfold curse of protection promised by God to Cain, and pronounces a 77-fold curse on anyone who killed him for committing the same act for which Cain was guilty-murder.

Seth's Lemach lived to the age of 777.[10]

Application

1. Who are you walking with? (See **4:22**)

SON OF BLESSED

Patriarch	line/age when born	years after son born	Age at death
Adam	Seth 130	800	930
Seth	Enos 105	807	912
Enos	Cainan 90	815	901
Cainan	Mahalaleel 70	840	910
Mahalaleel	Jared 65	830	895
Jared	Enoch 162	800	962
Enoch	Methuselah 65	300	365
Methuselah	Lamech 187	782	962
Lamech	Noah 182	595	777

Name of Patriarch	Meaning of the Name
Adam	man, ground
Seth	Compensation, granted
Enos	mortal man
Cainan	possessor
Mahalaleel	?
Jared	descent

Enosh	dedicated
Methuselah	when he is gone it will come
Lamech	powerful, overthrower
Noah	comfort, rest
Japheth	enlargement
Canaan-Kana	to be humble or subdued

WEEK FOUR
Genesis 6-9 The Flood

Day One

Observation

Genesis 6-Preparations for the Flood

1. a. What are we told about the sons of God and daughters of men in **verse 2**? (See also **Numbers 13:33**)

2. b. What did this result in? **(vs4)**

3. What does the Lord declare in **vs 3**?

4. What do we learn about the condition of man at this time? See **vs 5, 11-12.**

5. a. What is the Lord's response to this? See **vs 6-7.**
   b. What does the Lord decide to do? See also **vs 13.**
   c. What were four reasons for God's judgment?

6. Who found favor in the Lord's eyes? **(vs 8)**

7. What three things are we told about Noah? **(vs 9)**

8. a. How many sons did Noah have?
   b. Who were they?

9. What instructions does the Lord give to Noah?

10. What was it to be made from?

11. What was to be done to the inside and outside of it?

12. What were its dimensions supposed to be?

13. Why was Noah to do this?

14. What does the Lord tell Noah He was going to do with Noah and his family?

15. a. How many pairs of clean animals was he to bring with him?
    b. How many pairs of unclean animals was he to bring with him?
    c. How many pairs of the birds of the air was Noah to take with him?
    d. How was Noah to collect the animals? See **vs 20; 7:8-9,15.**

16. What else was Noah to bring with him on the ark?

17. What did Noah do?

18. a. How long did God wait to bring the flood? See **vs 3**
    b. Why do you think he waited so long?

Genesis 7-The Flood Cometh

1. Why did God save Noah and his family?

2. How many of every clean animal and birds was Noah to take?

3. How old was Noah when the floodwaters came upon the earth?

4. When did the flood of the earth begin?

5. What was the source of the floodwaters according to **vs 11**?

6. How long did the rain fall?

7. Who was on the ark with Noah?

8. a. Who shut the door of the ark?
   b. What does this symbolize?

9. How high did the waters rise?

10. What was the result of the flood?

11. How long did the waters flood the earth?

Genesis 8-A New World

1. What are we told God did in **verse 1**?

2. a. When did the ark come to rest?
   b. Where did it come to rest?

3. When did the tops of the mountains become visible?

4. What did Noah do forty days later?

5. a. What did Noah do seven days later?
   b. What happened?

6. a. What did Noah do seven days later?
   b. What happened?

7. When did Noah remove the covering of the ark?

8. When was the earth completely dry?

9. a. How did Noah know when to leave the ark?
   b. When did Noah and those with him leave the ark?

10. How long was Noah on the ark? See **7:11;8:14**.

11. a. What did Noah do when he left the ark?
    b. What was the Lord's reaction?

12. What promise does the Lord make?

13. What does **8:21** tell is about the inclinations of mans heart?

Day Two

Correlation

A. *Noah*
   1. a. What are we told about Noah in **Hebrews 11:7**?
      b. What according to this verse was Noah's attitude when preparing the ark.

   2. a. What does **2 Peter 2:5** tell us about Noah?
      b. What encouragement are we given from Noah's rescue by God in **2 Peter 2:9- 10**?

   3. What are we told in **Psalm 37:18-19** regarding the righteous?

B. *Man Fails to Listen*
   1. What does Jesus say concerning the days of Noah in the following verses? **Matthew 24:37-38 Luke 17:26-27**

2. What does **Psalm 104:6-9** tell us about the flood?

3. a. What warning does Peter give about scoffers in the last days in **2 Peter 3:3-4?**
   b. What do these scoffers deliberately forget according to **2 Peter 3:5-6?**

4. What does **1 Peter 3:19b-20** say about the people during Noah's time?

C. *God Sees*
   1. What do we learn about the Lord in the following verses?
      Job 28:24
      Job 31:4
      Job 34:21
      Psalm 11:4
      Psalm 33:13-15
      Psalm 139:1-4
      Proverbs 5:21
      Proverbs 15:3
      Jeremiah 16:17
      Jeremiah 17:10
      Jeremiah 32:19
      Hebrews 4:13

D. *Man's Wickedness*
   1. What are we told about man's wickedness in the following verses:
      Psalm 14:1-3
      Romans 3:23
      Isaiah 53:6
      Jeremiah 17:9

   2. What admonition does Jesus give in **John 8:34?**

E. *God's Patience*
1. What do we learn about God's patience in **2 Peter 3:9**?

2. What are we told in **James 3:2**?

3. What do we learn is God's desire in **1 Timothy 2:3-4**?

4. Which is the more dominant theme:
Judgment
Salvation

F. *God's Judgment*
1. What are we told in the following verses concerning the Lord judging the earth?
1 Chronicles 16:33
Psalm 9:8
Ecclesiastes 12:14
Acts 17:31

2. Whom are we told He will judge through according to **Romans 2:16?**

G. *Son's of God*
1. What do the following verses tell us concerning who the "sons of God" were?
Job 1:6
1 Peter 3:19-20
Jude 6

H. *Giants*
1. Nephiliam are also referred to in **Numbers 13:33**. What do we learn about them from this verse?

2. What giants are you facing?

I. Earth's Future Destruction

1. a. What does Peter warn about people who will come in the last days in **2 Peter 3:3,5**?
   b. What will they deliberately forget?

2. According to the following verses, how will the earth be destroyed in the future?
   Matthew 24:36-51
   Luke 17:26-36
   2 Peter 3:7,10,12

J. *Salvation*
   1. What does **1 Peter 3:20b-21** say concerning how Noah and those with him were saved?
   2. What does this water symbolize?

K. *Faith*
Faith deals with things unseen.
   1. What do we learn about faith from the following verses?
      Proverbs 4:23
      Proverbs 16:9
      Mark 7:21-23
      Luke 6:45

Word Wealth

Noah-means comfort or relief.

Ark-Hebrew tebah also used of the basket which Moses was placed in. See **Exodus 2:3,5.**

Nephilim-Hebrew word naphal means "fallen ones"

Shem-means "name" or "renoun"

Ham-means "hot"

Japheth-means "extend or enlargement"

strive-**vs 3** this is the only use of this word in the Old Testament. It is also translated as *contend, and abide.*

grief-**vs 6** Hebrew *nakham*- a deep, unfulfilled longing; deep pain and bitter anguish.[11]

grace-**vs 8** Hebrew *chen*-means favor, grace, graciousness, kindness, beauty, pleasantness, charm, attractiveness, loveliness, affectionate regard. Root *chanan* means "to act graciously or mercifully toward another, to be compassionate, to be favorably inclined.[12]

righteous-**vs 9** perfect- Hebrew *tamim*-sound, wholesome, having integrity

corrupt-**vs 11** spoiled, contaminated; changed from a sound condition to a deteriorated one; decayed.

destroy-**vs 13** blot out, utterly wipe out

covenant-**vs 18** Hebrew *berit* a compact, pledge, treaty, agreement, a binding and solomn agreement

This word is first used in **Genesis 6:18.**

wickedness-morally bad or wrong

evil-wicked, harmful

violence-Hebrew *khamas* refers to physical force used to injure, damage, or destroy. To do wrong, or be cruel, malicious, unjust, or oppressive in dealing with others.

Day Three

Commentary

Outline

A. Nephilim
B. Corrupt condition of the earth
C. God's grief and judgment pronounced
D. Noah
E. The Ark
    a. Building and preparations
    b. Entering

F. The Flood Cometh
    a. extent
    b. duration
    c. effects of

G. The ark comes to rest
    a. Noah sends out birds
    b. Leaving the Ark
    c. Building of an altar

H. A New Beginning

Genesis 6

vs 1-2 Some believe that "the sons of God" refer to fallen angels who left their proper dwelling places. We learn in **Matthew 22:30** and **Mark 12:25** that angels do not marry.

> For when the dead rise, they will neither marry nor be given in marriage. In this respect they will be like the angels in heaven. *Matthew 22:30* Also *Mark 12:25*.

Jude tells us of angels who failed to keep their own domain-they left their habitation- heaven.

> And I remind you of the angels who did not stay within the limits of authority God gave them but left the place where they belonged. God has kept them securely chained in prisons of darkness, waiting for the great day of judgment. ***Jude 6***

Another belief is that the "sons of God" refer to the descendants of Cain-the Godless race intermarrying with the descendants of Seth, the Godly line.

vs 3 120 years-it may have taken Noah this long to build the ark. Remember, there were no power tools in those days. This was the amount of time which the Lord was giving men of the earth to change their ways. The Lord is patient, and He desires man to repent, but God is righteous and must judge the wicked.

> The Lord is not slack concerning his promise, as some men count slackness; but is longsuffering to us-ward, not willing that any should perish, but that all should come to repentance.10 But the day of the Lord will come as a thief in the night; in the which the heavens shall pass away with a great noise, and the elements shall melt with fervent heat, the earth also and the works that are therein shall be burned up. ***2 Peter 3:9-10***

vs 5 Here we see that God sees the acts of man and judges them. We see just how far man had fallen-"*every* imagination of the thoughts of his heart were *only evil continually*"

vs 6 It grieved God to see how deprived His crown of creation had become.

vs 9 Here we learn three things about Noah:

1. He was a just man
2. He was blameless in his generation
3. He walked with God

Blameless here does not mean that he was sinless, but that he loved and obeyed the Lord.

Noah lived by faith in the midst of a wicked society.

We are told in **Deuteronomy 18:13** You shall be perfect with the Lord your God.

vs 10 Noah's sons-In **Genesis 5:32** we are told that Noah was 500 years old before he had these sons.

vs 15 The ark would have been 450 ft long, 75 ft wide, and 45 ft high. It would have been one and a half times the length of a football field, and as wide as half the length of a football field. It was six times longer than it was wide. This is the same ratio used by modern ship builders. It had three levels.

vs 18 Here is the first use of the word *covenant*. It was a formal binding contract between two parties. Noah's part was to follow God's instructions. God pledged to save Noah and all who were with him.

vs 22 Obedience to God is often contrary to the advice of the world.

7:1 Here we see God calling Noah to "come" enter the ark. It is an invitation which Noah had to choose to accept. Those who have accepted Christ will also receive an invitation to "come".

> And the Spirit and the bride say, Come. And let him that heareth say, Come. And let him that is athirst come. And whosoever will, let him take the water of life freely.
> ***Revelation 22:17***

7:2 God instructed Noah to take seven pairs of clean animals because they would be used for food after the flood. They would also be offered as sacrifices.

7:12 The flood occurred around 1656.

7:16 The Lord is the one who shut them in. This symbolized the fact that Noah could not save himself. Noah's faith was justified while earth's faithlessness was judged.

7:24 The flood waters were upon the earth for about five months.

A.   Earths Corrupt Condition

We find four reasons for God's judgment:
1. The great wickedness of man **Gen 6:5**
2. Every thought of men's heart was only evil continually **Gen 6:5**
3. The earth was corrupt-all flesh was corrupted **Gen 6:11**
4. The earth was filled with violence **Gen 6:11**

Genesis 7:1,4,7-10,16 Noah and his family enter the ark seven days prior to the flood. Perhaps it took them seven days to load the animals. People may have laughed at Noah's ark building project, but what were their thoughts when they saw the animals coming to Noah? Yet no one sought refuge. How stubborn the heart is.

B.   God

In this account we again see that God judges, but we also see His mercy shown toward Noah. He is just and holy.

We see that the decision to send the flood was a heart-wrenching decision for God. See **Gen 6:6**.

We also see that God is faithful and trustworthy- He keeps His promises.

He is the source of our life.

> ...when you take away Your breath they die and return to the dust. ***Psalm 104:29b*** See **Gen 6:3**.

Noah and his family are saved. Mankind has been salvaged. Salvaging involves retrieving that which is valuable from the wreckage. God is in the business of re-creating. We are saved from our sin and its condemnation; we are salvaged for ministry and service to God.[13]

C. Miscellaneous

7:20 The Geography of pre-flood times differed from today's geography.

We are not given any details concerning Noah's actual building of the ark. He had no power tools. Wood would have to be cut and hauled to the construction site. The author focuses only on Noah's obedience and completion of the Lord's directives.

The size of the ark was much greater than those of ancient sailing vessels. It wasn't until 1858 that a vessel of greater length was constructed-the Great Eastern which was 692 by 83 by 30 ft.[14]

Ararat-located in eastern Armenia, Turkey. Ararat is the highest peak at 17,000 ft.

raven-is a carrion eater.

olive trees-grow only at lower altitudes.

8:1 *God remembered Noah* This doesn't mean God had forgotten him, but that He expressed concern for him.

Noah was on the ark for 1 year and 10 days. We have no indication that God communicated with him during this time. Do you think Noah may have felt that God had abandoned him during this time?

Have you ever felt abandoned by the Lord?

8:11 dove and olive branches are both symbols of peace

8:15 This was one year and ten days after the rain started.

8:20 First use of the word *altar*.

Timeline for the Flood

> Second month, seventeenth day of Noah's 600th year-flood begins **Gen 7:11**
>
> Rained for forty days and forty nights **Gen 7:17**
>
> Seventh month seventeenth day of Noah's 600th year-ark comes to rest on Mount Ararat **Gen 8:4**

Water covered earth for 150 days **Gen 8:1**

> First day of tenth month-tops of mountains became visible **Gen 8:5**
>
> First month, first day of Noah's 601st year-water dried up from earth. Noah removed covering from the ark **Gen 8:13**
>
> Twenty-seventh day of the second month of Noah's 601st year-earth completely dry **Gen 8:14**

Noah vs Adam

Noah	Adam
obeyed God	disobeyed God
humanity blessed through	humanity cursed through

Food For Thought
Universality of Flood Tradition

Babylonians, Assyrians, Egyptians, Persians, Hindus, Greeks, Chinese, Phrygians, Fiji Islanders, Esquimaux, Aboriginal Americans, Indians, Brazilians, Peruvians, and every branch of the whole human race, Semitic, Aryan, Turanian all have traditions of a Great Deluge that destroyed all mankind, except one family.[15]

Archaeological Notes
The Flood Tablets

George Smith, of the British Museum, found (1872), in tablets from the Library of Assur- banipal at Ninevah, accounts of the flood which parallel the Biblical account, which had been copied from tablets dating back to the First Dynasty of Ur, a period about midway between the Flood and Abraham. Later many of these ancient tablets were found. In these tablets these expressions repeatedly occur: "The Flood," "the age before the Flood," "inscriptions of the time before the Flood."[16]

Flood Deposits

An Actual Layer of Mud, evidently deposited by the Flood, has been found in three separate places: Ur, Fara 60 miles further up the River, and Kish, 100 miles further up the river.

At Ur, City of Abraham, the Joint Expedition of the University Museum of Pennsylvania and the British Museum, under the leadership of Dr. C.L. Woolley, found (1929), near the bottom of the Ur mounds, underneath several strata of human occupation, a great bed of solid water-laid clay 8 feet thick without admixture of human relic, with yet the ruins of another city buried beneath it. Dr. Woolley said that 8 feet of sediment implied a very great depth and a long period of water, that it could not have been put there by any ordinary overflow of the rivers, but only by some such vast inundation as the Biblical Flood. The Civilization underneath the flood layer was so different from that above it that it indicated to Dr. Woolley "a sudden and terrific break in the continuity of history."[17]

Babylonian Noah's Own Story of the Flood

Part of what is known as the Gilgamesh Epic. Gilgamesh was the 5th king of the Erech dynasty, which was one of the first dynasties after the Flood. This Epic gives the story of his adventures, one of which was to visit the island abode of Utnapishtim, the Babylonian Noah. This visit is depicted on a seal which was recently found at Tell Billa near Ninevah. Utnapishtim relates the story of the Flood and his escape from it. In brief it is as follows: "The assembly of the gods decided to send a Deluge. They said, 'On the sinner let his sin rest.' O man of Shuruppak, build a ship, save your life. Construct it with six stories, each with seven parts. Smear it with bitumen inside and outside. Launch it upon the ocean. Take into the ship seed of life of every kind. I built it. With all that I had I loaded it, with silver, gold, and all living things that I had. I embarked upon the ship with my family and kindred. I closed the door. The appointed time arrived. I observed the appearance of the day. It was terrible. All light was turned to darkness. The rains poured down. The storm raged; like a battle charge on mankind. The boat trembled. The gods wept. I looked out upon the sea. All mankind was turned to clay, like logs floating about. The tempest ceased. The flood was over. The ship grounded on Mt. Zazir. On the seventh day I sent out a dove; it returned. I sent out a swallow; it returned. I sent out a raven; it alighted, it waded about; it croaked; it did not return. I disembarked. I appointed a sacrifice. The gods smelled the sweet savor. They said, "Let it be done no more."'[18]

The difference between the Gilgamesh Epic and the Biblical Noah is that in the Biblical account God destroyed the earth for a moral reason, not because He was inconvenienced or disturbed.

SUMMARY

From this account we learn that God takes sin seriously, and we should also.

Although Noah was surrounded by a wicked and evil generation, he made a choice to live a righteous life. We are told That Noah was

> "a righteous man, blameless among his generation, and he walked with God". **6:9**

We also live in a very sinful world, but we must try to live Godly lives.

Noah walked with God. He was completely obedient to God. God could have provided Noah with an ark or preserved him in some other way, but He gave Noah an opportunity to show faith and obedience.

When given instructions by God to build the ark, we are told that Noah was obedient.

> "he did everything that the Lord commanded Him." **6:22; 7:5**

Noah and his family were saved as all sinners are saved-by grace through faith, not through works. No one is saved because they deserve it. We are saved by the love and salvation which the Lord gives us even though we are so undeserving of it.

> For by grace are ye saved through faith; and that not of yourselves: it is the gift of God: 9 not of works, lest any man should boast. ***Ephesians 2:8-9***

The Lord established a covenant with him. **6:18; 9:9-17**

He was a farmer. **9:20**

He drank and became drunk. **9:21**

He was called a "preacher of righteousness". **2 Peter 2:5**

The Lord punishes sin when there is no repentance.

Just as the ark was the only means of escape, the only way of salvation is through Jesus Christ.

> Jesus saith unto him, I am the way, the truth, and the life: no man cometh unto the Father, but by me. ***John 14:6***

In this account we learn that God is a loving and holy God. Because He is holy He must judge sin. He expresses wrath against the unrepentant. Because He is a God of love, He is patient, merciful and forgiving of those who repent and turn to Him.

We learn that God sees all-the good and the bad.

Noah's Righteousness		World's Unrighteousness	
Found grace in god's eyes	6:8	Great wickedness on earth	6:5
Was a just man	6:9	Man's every thought was evil	6:5
Was perfect in his generation	6:9	Earth was corrupt	6:11-12
Walked with God	6:9	Earth full of violence	6:11,13
God established covenant with	6:18	Ungodly	2 Peter 2:5

Did all God commanded him	6:22		
Saved his house	Heb 11:7		
Was a preacher of righteousness	2 Peter 2:5		

In **2 Peter 2:5** Noah is called "a preacher of righteousness". Imagine how discouraged he must have been to have not been able to gain any converts.

Application

What obedience is God asking of you today?

Day Four

Observation

Genesis 9-Noahic Covenant

1. What did the Lord do to Noah and his sons?

2. a. What instruction does God give to Noah and his family in **vs 1, 7**??
   b. Compare this with Genesis 1:28.

3. a. What does the Lord give to them for food at this point?
   b. What condition is given concerning this food?

4. What is the punishment God prescribes for murder?

5. a. What covenant does the Lord make?
   b. Who was the covenant with?

    c. What type of covenant was this, conditional or unconditional?
    d. What was the duration of the covenant?

6. What was the sign of the covenant?

7. What was Noah's occupation?

8. What did Noah do?

9. a. What happened while Noah was in this condition?
    b. Who was informed about this?
    c. What did they do?

10. a. What did Noah do when he found out what had happened while he was asleep?
    b. What did this consist of?

11. How old was Noah when he died?

Correlation

A. Instructions Regarding Murder
killed-Hebrew harag-means to slaughter.

Premeditated, intentional slaying of another person.

See Exodus 20:13; Leviticus 24:17

murder vs manslaughter See **Exodus 21:12-14**

B. Instructions Concerning Blood
    1. What are we told in **Leviticus 17:11** that blood was to be used for?
    2. What are we told in **Hebrews 9:22**?

- C. Animals
    1. a. What did the Lord say about man's relationship with the animals in **vs 2**.
       b. What will the relationship with animals be like in the ultimate restoration of God's kingdom? See **Isaiah 11:6-9**.
- D. Rainbow
    1. What are we told is around the Lord's throne in **Revelation 4:3?**

Outline

- A. New Beginning
- B. God Institutes Government
- C. Noahic Covenant
- D. The Sign of the Covenant
- E. Noah's Sons
- F. Noah's Indiscretion
- G. Canaan Cursed

Commentary

vs 1-2 This is reminiscent of the instruction God gave in **Genesis 1:28**. In the garden man had been given every seed bearing plant for food. Here they are given meat-fowl, and fish to eat.

vs 5 Here we are given a mandate from God for capital punishment. Many today are opposed to the death penalty, but it is mandated by God Himself.

God would not take the guilty person's life, it was to be the responsibility of people to see that judgment was carried out.

vs 13 David Atkinson tells us that the Hebrew term qeshat used to describe the rainbow is the term normally used for the bow of a warrior. The hostility is over-God hangs up His bow.[19]

vs 21 After sin entered the world, nakedness was associated with shame.

Notice that it wasn't during a time of trial that Noah fell, but during a time of ease. We need to be on our guard at all times, because we never know when temptation will present itself.

> So, if you think you are standing firm, be careful that you don't fall! *1 Corinthians 10:12*

We see here from Noah's actions that man was still in a fallen state and would still sin. Evil was still present.

Day Five

Observation

Genesis 10-Noah's Descendants

1. a. How many sons did Japheth have?
   b. Who were they?

2. a. How many sons did Ham have?
   b. Who were they?

3. a. Who was the father of Nimrod?
   b. What are we told about Nimrod?

4. What territory did Nimrod have in his kingdom?

5. What were the borders of Canaan?

6. Who were the two sons born to Eber?

7. What happened in the days of Peleg?

8. a. How many sons did Shem have?
   b. Who were they?

9. Where did the Schemites live?

10. How old was Shem at the time of the flood?

The geographic area in this chapter reaches from the Iranian plateau in the east, the Mediterranean coastlands in the west, the Black Sea in the north and Somolia in Africa in the South.

All nations and peoples came from Noah's descendants.

Genesis 11-The Tower of Babel

1. What are we told about the world at this point?

2. Where did the people settle?

3. a. What project did they propose?
   b. What was the purpose of this project?

4. What did they use for building materials?

5. What two things did the Lord do?

6. a. What was the tower called?
   b. What does this name mean?

7. How old was Shem at the time of the flood?

8. a. What are we told in **Acts 17:26**?
   b. What reason did He do this? See **Acts 17:27**

9. Who were the children of Terah?

10. a. Who was Haran the father of? see **11:27,29**
    b. What happened to Haran?

11. Who did Abram and Nahor marry?

12. What are we told about Sarai?

13. Where did Terah head to?

14. Who did he take with him?

15. Where did they end up?

16. How old was Terah when he died?.

Name	Age when son born	begat	Age lived to
Shem	100	Araphaxad	600
Araphaxad	35	Salah	438
Salah	30	Eber	433
Eber	34	Peleg	464
Peleg	30	Reu	239
Reu	32	Serug	239
Serug	30	Nahor	230
Nahor	29	Terah	148
Terah	70	Abram, Nahor, Haran	205

Commentary

Outline
Genesis 10

A. Japhites-**vs 2-4**

B. Hamites-**vs 6-13**
    a. Nimrod-**vs 8-12**
    b. Canaanites **vs 15-18**
    c. Shemites **vs 21-29**

Chapter 10 Table of Nations

In this chapter 70 descendants of Noah are listed.

2-5 14 descendants of Japheth. His descendants became the Indo-European people who settled parts of Asia, Europe, and Spain.

6-18 30 descendants are recorded for Ham, 11 of which are for the Canaan branch. They settled in North Africa and the Far East.

Nimrod was a mighty hunter and a city builder. The name comes from Karad which means to rebel or to be rebellious. Mighty hunter before the Lord may have meant that he was a hunter of men, a conqueror, and that he stood against the Lord. He built a kingdom of cities-Babel, Erech, Accad, Calneh were located in the land of Shinar. Erech was the capital of ancient Sumeria, the location of the oldest written records known to man-cuneform.

Nineveh, Rehoboth and Calah were located in Assyria. Ninevah was the future capital of the Assyrian empire.

This area was located in what today is known as Palestine, Arabia and Egypt. It stretched from the Northern Tigris to the southern Euphrates-about 400 miles.

Rehobothir may be ancient Asshur.[20]

Out of Casluhim came Philistim who was the descendant of the Philistines.

Canaan was the ancestor of the Canaanites which included the Hittites, Amorites, Jebusites, and Hivites among others.

vs 19 The border of the Canaanites was from Sidon toward Gerar, as far as Gaza, toward Sodom and Gomorrah, Adamah and Zeboiim as far as Lasha. They were the inhabitants of the cities of Sodom and Gomorrah.

Thirty nations came from Ham's descendants.

21-31 Genealogy of Shem-chosen line. Here 26 names are listed. See also **11:10-26** which gives fewer names but gives chronological data as well. This list connects Noah to Abraham.

They became the Hebrews and Syrians.

Chapter 11 Tower of Babel

A. The Tower of Babel

B. Abraham's Descendants

vs 3 This is the first significant building project in the Bible since the flood.

The people propose a building project so they could "make a name for ourselves". Here they are showing pride and arrogance. They aren't concerned with God's glory, but their own glory.

They are attempting to reach God in their own way. It might also have been an attempt to say they didn't need God.

The material they used to build the tower was not simply rocks, but bricks which they made. The tower was probably a ziggurat-a step pyramid.

vs 5 Even though they built "a tower with its top in the sky" God still had to "come down". We see from this that God is interested in what man does. He didn't send an angel to make a report, but He Himself came "to see".

vs 6 What did the Lord see? Prideful man who was depending upon themselves and not God. When we rely on ourselves and not upon God, evil results.

vs 8-9 The actions of the men resulted in God's judgment. The men were rebelling against God's instructions to "fill the earth". They wanted power and control. By confusing their language, they were unable to communicate and so were forced to scatter. On the day of Pentecost, the Holy Spirit allowed the apostles to speak different languages so they were able to communicate the gospel to "the ends of the earth".

> On the day of Pentecost all the believers were meeting together in one place. 2 Suddenly, there was a sound from heaven like the roaring of a mighty windstorm, and it filled the house where they were sitting. 3 Then, what looked like flames or tongues of fire appeared and settled on each of them. 4 And everyone present was filled with the Holy Spirit and began speaking in other languages, as the Holy Spirit gave them this ability. ***Acts 2:1-4***

11:9 *Babylon-*In Scripture this city represents human, political, economic and religious systems which are devoted to materialism and ungodly living in defiance to the holiness and sovereignty of God.

Ruins of the ancient city lie along the River Euphrates, about 50 miles south of Bagdad in modern Iraq. At its zenith the city covered about six square miles.

Herodotus writing in the fifth century B.C. states that the city was surrounded by 609 miles of walls up to 300 ft high and 87 ft wide.[21]

11:31 *Ur of Chaldees-*This city was dominated by a giant three-stage ziggurat, reaching some 70 feet above the flat plain. It worshipped the moon god Nunnar. The city was enclosed by oval walls some 30 feet high, which protected the city and two harbors. Streets were carefully laid out. Archaeology had discovered gold jewelry, gold-inlaid musical objects, and colorful mosaics illustrating civil and military life. A number of clay tablets were recovered, including a Sumerian dictionary and a mathematical text recording square roots. Business records show that the city was actively involved in international trade.[22]

Terah may have left Ur because of the destruction by the Elamites in 1950 B.C.

Word Wealth

Nimrod- Hebrew marad means revolt.

He founded four cities in Shinar-tip of Persian Gulf. He was the first kingdom builder.

He went to Assyria and built Ninevah, Rehoboth ir, Calah, and Resen, which was between Ninevah and Caleh.

Ninevah and Caleh both served as capitals of Assyria. Ninevah endured until 612 B.C.

Archaelogical excavations have established that Ninevah's beginnings can be traced back at least to 5,000 B.C.

*plain of Shinar-*about 50 miles south of present day Bagdad.

*Ur of Chaldeans-*Summerian commercial center on the Euphrates in southern Mesopotamia. It had a population of about 300,000.

It worshipped the sun god Nanna. Its culture included mathematics, weaving, and astrology.

Babel- became capital of Babylonia. Hebrew balal means "to confuse". Can also mean "gate of the God". This later became the city of Babylon, which eventually becomes the fountainhead of demon worship, and in Revelation it becomes synonymous with the city that persecutes God's people. It symbolizes worldly pride, moral corruption, and defiance against God. It represents the world system that rebels against God.[23]

tower-migdal- appears in Scripture as a symbol of pride.

sons of Shem-From his descendants came the monotheistic religions-Islam, Judaism, Christianity.

*Elam-***10:22** sired the Elamites-dwelled east of the Tigris.

*Lud-***10:22** Lydians of Asia Minor

*Aram-***10:23** Syrian people known as Armeans

*Arphaxad-***see 10:24;11:11-12**

*Peleg-***10:25** means divided

*Haran-***11:31** in northern Mesopotamia. Approximately 600miles north of Ur.

From Ur to Canaan was 1500 miles.

Application

Are you guilty of self sufficiency instead of depending on God?

Food For Thought

According to the ages given in these genealogies:

    It was 1656 years from Adam to the Flood.

    427 years from the Flood to Abraham.

Adam's life overlapped Methuselah by 243 years.

Methuselah's life overlapped Noah by 600 years-died the year of the Flood.

There were 126 years between the death of Adam and the birth of Noah.

Noah lived 350 years after the Flood; died 2 years before the birth of Abraham.

Shem lived from 98 years before the Flood to 502 years after the Flood. Shem lived to 75 years after Abraham entered Canaan.[24]

WEEK FIVE

Day One

Genesis 12 Call of Abram

Observation

1. What instructions did God give Abraham?

2. What promises did God make to Abram?

3. a. What is Abram's response to the Lord's instruction?
   b. How old was Abram when he left Haran?

4. a. Who did Abram take with him?
   b. How do you think the persons involved feel about this?

5. Where did Abram go?

6. Who was living the land?

7. What did the Lord tell Abram while he was here?

8. What did Abram do?

9. Where did Abram then go?

10. What did he do there?

11. What problem did Abram encounter?

12. Where did Abram go because of this?

13. What did Abram fear?

14. a. What request did Abram make of Sarai?
    b. What does this action say about Abram?

15. What happened to Sarah?

16. What did the Lord do?

17. What did Pharaoh do?

18. Mark all the "I will" statements in this chapter.

Key Places

vs 4 *Haran*-in northern Mesopotamia. It is about 600 miles north of Ur.

vs 6 *Shechem*-Means "shoulder". It is located on slope of Mount Ebal. This was the first city in Canaan Abraham visited.

It is the site of an alter built by Jacob called El Elohe Israel which means "God, the God of Israel. Jacob purchased a parcel of land for 100 pieces of silver.

great tree of Moreh-Moreh means teacher.

vs 8 *Bethel*-Means "house of God". Place where Abraham built an altar. It is twenty miles south of Shechem in what is modern Beitin.

Here we see Abraham worshipping the Lord. He "called on the name of the Lord" meaning he made proclamation concerning God to the heathens living in the land. This is central to worship and witness.

This is where Abraham returns to after going to Egypt. It was originally called Luz (**Genesis 28:19**)

It is 12 miles north of Jerusalem.

It was the location where Jacob erected pillar to mark dream of angels ascending and descending a ladder. (**Genesis 28:10-22**)

It was home of the Ark of the Covenant in the period of judges. (**Judges 20:26-27**)

Ai-means ruin. See **Joshua 7** for when Israelites defeat this town.

Correlation

A. Abram's Call

It has been about 400 years since the flood.

God appears to Abraham. God is seeking Abraham, it does not appear that Abraham was looking for God. We don't know in what form this encounter took place. It was possibly a dream.
1. What does **Nehemiah 9:7-8** tell us about God's calling Abraham?

2. What are we told in **Joshua 24:2-3**?

This may be one reason why God instructed Abram to "leave...your father's household". What would cause Abram to follow this God? Ur worshipped Nunnar-the moon god.

Note that God sought Abram. It doesn't appear that Abram was seeking God.
3. What does **Acts 7:2-4** tell us about when the Lord called Abram?

4. What are we told in **Romans 3:11**?

vs 3 ...all peoples on earth will be blessed through you-ultimately, Abram would be the descendant of the Messiah-Jesus.
    5.   What are we told about this in **Galatians 3:7-8,14?**

vs 4 We don't know how much time Abram wasted in Haran. We know that Terah was 205 years old when he died-see **Gen 11:32**. Abram at this point was 75. We don't know if Abram left immediately upon his father's death.

vs 5 We are not told anything about the journey, or how long it took. From Haran, it is about 900 miles.
    6.   What are we told about Abram's actions in **Hebrews 11:8**?

Abram's actions show that he:
    1.   trusted divine guidance
    2.   believed the divine promises.

7.   was living "by faith and not by sight"-see **2 Corinthians 5:7.**
    a.   Just as Abram was called by God, we also have a calling.
    b.   What did Jesus say in **Mark 10:29-30** that we do for the gospel's sake?
    c.   What will be the result of doing this?
    d.   What final instructions does Jesus give? See **Mark 16:15; Matthew 28:19-20.**
    e.   What are we warned against in **James 4:4; 1 John 2:15?**
    f.   What does James tell us in **James 1:27?**

B.   *Abraham in Egypt*

    1.   What are we told about friendship with the world in **James 4:4?**

Commentary

A. *The Lord Again Appears to Abram*

The Lord tells Abram that this is the land he will receive.

Notice that the Lord doesn't communicate with Abram again until Abram has obeyed the first instructions that he had been given by the Lord.

Abram responds to the Lord by building an altar.

Abram continues to explore the land and builds another altar and calls on the name of the Lord. This is a witness to the Canaanites who are living in the land.

B. *Calling on the Name of Yahweh*

This we will see was a practice of Abraham's. See also **13:4; 21:33**.

C. *Abram in Egypt*

Abram is faced with a famine in the land, and instead of seeking God's direction, he decides to go to Egypt. This is another 300 mile trip.

We are to walk by faith, not our feelings. When Abram felt fear, he reacted based on his feelings.

Egypt is a picture of the world. Abram had to learn that walking with the Lord meant separation from the things of the world.

We are not told how long Abram was in Egypt, but he was not in God's will while he was down there.

vs 18-19 We don't know how Pharaoh came to the knowledge that Sarai was Abram's wife.

D. Fear

Abram is fearful that he will be killed because Sarai is so beautiful, so he says that Sarai is his sister.

Lying is usually the result of fear.

This shows a lack of trust in the Lord's ability to protect him. When we take matters into our own hands, we tend to start getting ourselves in trouble. We also often miss experiencing God's provision.

How should we deal with fear?
1. Go to the Lord in prayer.
2. Trust that the Lord is in control.
3. Seek God in His word.

E. The Lord's Protection

Abram's relationship with the Lord is new, and he doesn't have the Bible to look to as we do. This experience will show Abram that he can rely on the Lord.

The Lord sends plagues on Pharaoh and his household because of Abram's wife Sarai.

F. Poor Witness

vs 20 *sent*-Hebrew shalakl

Unfortunately here Pharaoh is seen to have more integrity than Abram. Abram's actions result in a poor witness for the Lord.

Abraham's deception resulted in his being sent away in shame and disgrace. He is rebuked by a heathen.

This foreshadows when Pharaoh would send Moses and the Israelites out of Egypt-see **Ex 12:31**

Vocabulary

Negev-dry wasteland stretching southward from Beersheba to Kadesh Bernea, and east and west from the Mediterranean Sea to the Arabah-about 70 miles.

About 50 miles south of Bethel.

Means dry. Same Hebrew word is also translated "south" in **Genesis 13:14.**

bless-speaking and delivering good into someones life.

Application

When have you been in a situation where you are following God's direction but were then faced with an unexpected trial? What was the outcome?

When have you been in a situation where you took matters into your own hands instead of seeking God's guidance? What was the outcome?

SUMMARY

Note that the Lord never initially promises to give anything to Abram. He only promises to bless him and make his name great. Abram does not know where he is going. The Lord only tells him to "go to a land I will show you." see **vs 1.**

At this point Abram doesn't know anything about God. He was originally a moon worshipper. See **Joshua 24:2**. Abraham followed God without any idea of where God was leading him. God had made

Abram a promise and Abram trusted God would keep His promise and so he acted in faith. Imagine how he might have felt. Imagine how Sarai may have felt. They get to the land, and God confirms with Abram that He will give his offspring the land.

Abram next faces his first test. Imagine how he and Sarai must have felt when they encountered a famine. They probably had fears and perhaps doubted if they had taken the right action in obeying the Lord. After all God had promised blessings not hardship.

God often uses circumstances to test His people and reveal Himself to them.

Obedience leads to new assurance and new promises from God. Warren Wiersbe says that tests often follow triumphs. We must continually walk in obedience.[25]

At this point Abram is acting out of fear. He is in a strange land surrounded by foreigners. He fears the famine and the foreigners. When he entered the land, He worshipped God, but his relationship with God is in its early stages. He hasn't yet figured out that God is faithful and will take care of him. He hasn't yet developed faith and dependence on God. Many times one bad choice snowballs into other bad choices. Abram made the wrong choice to depend on himself instead of God and this led to other poor choices. It was only because of God's faithfulness that those choices didn't result in disastrous consequences.

Fear and faith cannot co-exist. George Muller said, "The beginning of anxiety is the end of faith; and the beginning of true faith is the end of anxiety."

When we are not following God, He sometimes uses difficult circumstances or even the rebuke of an ungodly person to get us back on the right path.[26]

When we make choices out of the flesh, choosing our way instead of relying on God's guidance, we often loose the blessing God would like to bestow on us, or end up in a situation which God would have protected us from if we had followed His direction.

> Trust in the Lord with all your heart and lean not on your own understanding; in all your ways acknowledge Him and He will make your paths straight. *Proverbs 3:5-6*

Imagine the fear-terror Sarah must have felt when she was taken into Pharaoh's palace. How do you think she felt toward her husband at this point?

How do you think she felt when Pharaoh's household was inflicted with serious diseases? Did she associate them with the hand of God?

I wonder how Pharaoh found out that Sarai was Abram's wife.

Day Two

Abram and Lot
Genesis 13 Abram and Lot Separate

Observation

1. Where did Abram go from Egypt?

2. What do we learn about Abram?

3. Where did Abram finally return to?

4. What did Abram do there?

5. What happens between Lot and Abram's herdsmen?

6. Who else were living there at that time?

7. What does Abram suggest?

8. How is the plain of Jordan described?

9. What did Lot choose?

10. What are we told about the men of Sodom?

11. What happens when Lot left?

12. What promise does the Lord make here?

13. Where does Abram move next?

14. What does Abram do there?

Commentary

God blessed Abram with wealth, even though Abram wasn't in God's will.

vs 3-4 Abram is again in God's will, and by calling on the name of the Lord he is showing his dependence upon the Lord. When we fail, Satan often tries to tell us we should quit and give up. We need to return to the Lord. If we allow Him to, God can even use our failures to achieve His purposes.

> And we know that all things work together for good to them that love God, to them who are the called according to his purpose. **Romans 8:28**

vs 7 Because other people were also living in the land with their herds, the land would become stressed if too many herds were in one area. Also Abraham's actions would be viewed by these foreigners. We must always be aware that unbelievers are watching our actions.

vs 10-Notice that Lot
  looks
  saw
  chose-for himself the best portion.

As the eldest, Abram would have had the right to make the first choice. Here we see that Abram doesn't want strife in his family.

vs 11 Lot journeyed eastward-east symbolizes moving away from God and His blessing. See **Genesis 3:24; 4:16; 11:2**

vs 13 Here we receive a foreshadowing of things to come.

vs 14 Here Abram is given a third promise from the Lord.

Word Wealth

Lot means "concealed or covering."

quarreling-Hebrew meribah means conflict or strife.

Hebron-originally called Kiriath-Arba located just north of the Negev. Name means communion. It was located approximately 25 miles southwest of city which was later known as Jerusalem, and was less than two miles from Mamre.

Genesis 14 Araham Rescues Lot
Observation

1. List the kings and the cities they were king of in **verses 1-2.**

2. Where were the following living?
   Rephaites
   Zuzites
   Emites
   Horites
   Amalekites and Amorites

3. Who did Chedorlaomer and the kings allied with him defeat?

4. Where did the battle of the kings take place?

5. What are we told about the Valley of Siddim?

6. Who won the battle?

7. What did the victors do?

8. a. What did Abraham do when he heard about his nephew?
   b. How many men were with Abraham?
   c. Who were allied with Abram?

9. What happened?

10. a. Who came out to meet Abram when he returned?
    b. Where did they meet Abram?

11. a. What are we told about Melchizedek?
    b. What does his name mean?

12. What did Melchizedek bring?

13. What did Abram give to Melchizedek?

14. Who did Melchizedek say was responsible for Abram's victory?

15. By what name do Melchizedek and Abram call God?

16. What offer did the king of Salem make?

17. What was Abram's response?

Correlation

The following passages compare Jesus as our high priest to Melchizedek.

1. a. What has the Lord sworn according to **Psalm 110:4**?
   b. Who is this verse referring to?

Read **Hebrews 5:1-6**

2. What are we told about the high priest in **Hebrews 5:1-4**, concerning his selection, and duties?

3. What does **Hebrews 5:5-6** say regarding Jesus?

4. What does **Hebrews 6:20** say concerning Jesus and Melchizedek?

Read **Hebrews 7:1-17**.

5. What are we told about Melchizedek in **vs 2**?

6. How is Melchizedek compared to Jesus in **vs 3**?

7. What was unusual about the fact that Abraham paid tribute to Melchizedek according to **vs 5-6**?

8. What did the fact that Abraham paid tribute to Melchizedek show?

9. Why was it necessary for a new priesthood that was different from that of the Levitical one? See **vs 11**.

10. How does Jesus' priesthood differ from that of the Levitical priesthood? **vs 16**.

Commentary

Here is recorded the first war in Scripture.

vs 1-King of Shinar...this is Babylon, the place of the tower in **Genesis 11. vs 18** Melchizedek represented our Lord's priesthood.

Melchizedek appears out of nowhere, and has no lineage. Jesus himself as God has no beginning or end.

Jesus' priesthood is not based upon ancestry, but upon the power of an indestructible life. His priesthood is greater than that of the Levitical priesthood because:

1. He does not need to offer sin offerings on His behalf-see **Hebrews 7:27**
2. He is "holy, blameless, pure, set apart from sinners"-see **Hebrews 7:26.**
3. He does not need to make continual sacrifices-see **Hebrews 7:27.**
4. He lives forever to make intercession on our behalf and will never require a successor- see **Hebrews 21,24.**

vs 15 Mamre to Damascus was 240 miles.[27]

Vocabulary

Shinar-where tower of Babal was built-see **Gen 11:2.** Is in modern day Iraq.

Bera-means "in evil"

Birsha-means "in wickedness"

Elam-is in Persia

Salem-means "peace" This became Jerusalem.

Melchizadek-means king of righteousness

El Elyon-God Most High-refers to God's absolute sovereignty. Elyon is derived from *Alah* which means "to ascend". Elyon means uppermost, supreme, lofty, exalted, elevated.[28]

"possessor of heaven and earth" **vs 19**-means God is supreme, exalted.

Dan- also known as Laish. North of lake Galilee.

Hobah- 60 miles north of Damascus.

Dan was 40 miles north of Damascus

vs 20 This is the first time we see the practice of a tithe. See **Leviticus 27:30-32; Numbers 18:21-30.**

vs 22-23 Here Abram shows his dependance on God alone.

Day Three

Genesis 15 Cutting a Covenant

Observation

1. How does the Lord refer to Himself in **verse 1**?

2. What does Abram call the Lord? **vs 2**

3. What is Abram's concern?

4. What does the Lord tell Abram?

5. What is Abram's response to this?

6. How does the Lord receive Abram's response?

7. What instructions does the Lord give to Abram in **vs 9**?

8. What does the Lord tell Abram in **vs 13-16**?

9. What is the form which the Lord is seen here?

10. Why wasn't Abram given the land at this point-**vs 16**?

11. What did the covenant consist of?

Correlation

A. *Abram's faith*

Read **Galatians 3:6-9, 14**
1. What does Paul say about believers?
2. What does Paul say about Gentiles?
3. What does Paul say here was announced in advance to Abraham?
4. What does Paul say about faith in **verse 14**?

Read **Romans 4:1-5,13-22**
5. What do these verses say regarding how Abraham was justified?

6. What does **verse 4** say concerning a man's works?

7. What are we told that God does?

8. a. What are we told in **vs 5** is required to have a person's faith credited as righteousness?
   b. What is it not based on?

9. What are we told in **vs 13** concerning the promise? It was not through_____but through_____.

10. According to **vs 14**, what is the result if those who are of the law are heirs?

11. According to **vs 16**, why is the promise by faith?

12. What does **vs 17** say that God does?

13. What did Abraham not waver in?

Read **Romans 3:21-22**

14. a. What is the source of righteousness?
    b. Who testifies to this?

15. How is righteousness received?

16. What according to **Hebrews 11:1** is faith?

17. What do we learn in **Hebrews 11:6** concerning faith?

18. What are we told in **Romans 8:25** concerning hope?

B. *The Lord is a Shield*
   1. What do the following verses state about the Lord?
      2 Samuel 22:31
      Psalm 3:3
      Psalm 5:12
      Psalm 18:2
      Psalm 28:7
      Psalm 33:20
      Psalm 84:11
      Proverbs 30:5

Commentary
Outline

I. Abraham is encouraged by God.
II. Abraham questions God.
III. The Lord Confirms His Promise
IV. Abraham believes God

vs 1 We don't know how old Abram is at this point.

This is Abram's fourth encounter with the Lord. Here the Lord tells Abram that He will be Abram's shield and reward. This is in response to Abram turning down any of the plunder from his rescue of Lot. It is a promise of protection and provision.

vs 2 Sovereign Lord-Adonai

God again promises Abram he will father a son, and Abram responds with belief.

Eliezar means God of help

vs 6 This is not based on Abraham's sinlessness, but because of his faith.

Because Abram believed that the Lord was :
    willing
    able

to do what He promised, the Lord counted Abram as righteous. God added up everything that Abraham's faith meant to him and after considering it all together, determined it to be equal to righteousness.

Abraham leaned wholly on the promise of God and the God of promise.

Hope is to wish or long for something. True faith is not based on evidence of our senses, but on the character of God. We have faith because we trust God will do what He says He will do because He can do it and is willing to do it.[29]

vs 16 ...the sin of the Amorites has not yet reached its full measure. We are told of the Lord's great patience.

> The Lord is not slack concerning his promise, as some men count slackness; but is longsuffering to us-ward, not willing that any should perish, but that all should come to repentance. **2 Peter 3:9**

vs 17 *smoking firepot and flaming torch...* Fire represents the Lord's cleansing, consuming zeal and unapproachable holiness.

God revealed Himself to Moses as a burning bush-**Exodus 3:2**.

As the Israelites traveled through the wilderness, the Lord appeared as a pillar of fire by night.-**Exodus 13:21-22**.

When God met with the people on Mount Sinai, He appeared as fire-**Exodus 19:18**.

Vocabulary

shield-Hebrew magen

heir- Hebrew ben-mesheq son of possession.

Lord-Yahweh-He who causes (everything else) to be.[30]

believe-to make firm, to stand firm, to be enduring, to trust. To lean your whole weight upon.

accounted-(chashab) to think, reckon, to put together, imagine, impute, calculate, lay one's thoughts together- The consideration of a number of elements and draw a conclusion based on a wide overview, to form a judgement, to devise, to plan, to produce something in the mind.[31]

righteousness-a right relationship with God, which erases the believers guilt.

cutting a covenant

The Lord is the only one to walk between the pieces. He appears in the form of a smoking firepot with a blazing torch. Walking between the cut pieces was stating that should the person not keep their promise, may the same thing happen to them that happened to the animals they were walking between.

> The men who have violated my covenant and have not fulfilled the terms of the covenant they made before me, I will treat like the calf they cut in two and then walked between its pieces. ***Jeremiah 34:18***

faith-confidence, reliance, belief, especially without evidence or proof; based on testimony or authority.[32]

nations

Jebusites-lived in Jerusalem

Perizzites-means villager-lived in central Palestine

Hittites-kingdom north of Palestine-modern day Turkey.

Amorites-Central hill country of Palestine

Canaanites-descendants of Ham's son Canaan.

SUMMARY

Abraham's faith was based entirely upon God's character-His faithfulness.

Faith shows that we trust God. Our faith gives evidence to the world of things not seen-see **Hebrews 11:1.**

Day Four

Genesis 16 Abram and Hagar

Observation

1. a. What suggestion does Sarai make to Abram?
   b. What does this suggest?

2. What is Abram's response?

3. How long has Abram and Sarai been living in Canaan at this point?

4. How does Hagar react when she conceives?

5. How does Sarai respond to Hagar's pregnancy?

6. What does Abram tell Sarai?

7. What does Sarai then do?

8. What does Hagar do in response to Sarai's actions?

9. a. Who finds Hagar?
   b. Where is she?

10. What two questions does the angel ask Hagar?

11. What is Hagar's answer?

12. What instructions is Hagar given?

13. What promise is Hagar given?

14. What information about her child is Hagar given?

15. What name does Hagar give to the Lord?

16. Where is the well located?

17. a. How old is Abram when Ishmael is born?
    b. How long had he been waiting for God's promise to be fulfilled? (see **Gen12:4**)

18. What does the name Ishmael mean?

Application

1. How long have you been waiting for the fulfillment of a promise from God?

2. What situation are you in that you think the Lord does not see?

Remember that the Lord is El Roi, the God who sees.

For Further Study

Do a concordance search on see, saw, hears. See how many times the Bible tells us the Lord sees and hears when people cry out to him.

Commentary

vs 1-2 Barrenness was seen as a divine punishment, or a sign of divine displeasure.

The Lord has kept me from having children... Is Sarah showing resentment here? Imagine the anguish Sarah must have felt in making this sacrifice. She has no idea of the consequences of her actions. They have been felt throughout history. Children are a reward from the Lord.

> Sons are a heritage from the Lord, children a reward from Him. **Psalm 127:3**

Sarah at this point is not acting out of faith, but human reasoning-rationalization. Before we jump to condemn her, we need to remember that she didn't know the end of the story as we do. Remember Sarai and Abram have been living in Canaan now for ten years. Sarah is now 76 years old, and Abram is 85 years old. Sarai has probably experience menopause.

How long have you been waiting for an answer to prayer?

We need to remember that God doesn't work on our time scale. When we start looking at things from our perspective we usually end up making wrong decisions.

Apparently Abram does not consult the Lord about his decision, and apparently doesn't disagree at all with Sarah but eagerly agrees.

What Sarai proposed was a common practice. Archaeologists have discovered tablets containing marriage contracts which "specify that a barren wife must provide a woman for her husband for the purpose of procreation".[33]

vs 4-6 We don't know how old Hagar is.

She becomes pregnant and then begins to despise her mistress. She becomes haughty and arrogant.

Some of this may have been in part due to Sarah being oversensitive and jealous, and frustration over the fact that she is unable to bear children.

We see Sarai's pain and how desperate she is not only to have a child, but to please her husband.

Sarai then turns to Abram and blames him for Hagars treatment, even though she was the one who proposed the plan to begin with. This is an indication of the inner turmoil and pain she was experiencing.

Strife is often the result when we take matters into our own hands.

Some of the problem may have stemmed from Sarah's perception and jealousy. Sarah treats Hagar harshly and Hagar runs away.

Sarah acts, accuses and is angry.

Trials bring out either the best or worst in us. In this trial we see Sarai's desperation, lack of faith, jealousy and even meanness in her harsh treatment of Hagar. We also see Hagar's arrogance and hatred. Jesus said that our words reflect our heart.

> For out of the overflow of the heart the mouth speaks. The good man brings good things out of the good stored up in him, and the evil man brings evil things out of the evil stored up in him. **Matthew 12:34b-35**

F.B. Meyer says "If our lot is hard and our cross is heavy we start off in a fit of impatience and wounded pride. We must retrace our steps and meekly bend our necks under the yoke. We must accept the lot that God has ordained for us, even though it may be the result of the cruelty and sin of others."[34]

vs 7-9

Road to Shur-Shur is about 150 miles from Palestine toward Egypt.

Apparently Hagar was planning on returning to Egypt.

Here we have the first use of the word angel.

This is believed to be a theophany, or an appearance of the preincarnate Christ. We know that it is God appearing here and not just an angel because we are told in **verse 13** *the Lord who spoke to her.*

Note that the angel calls Hagar by name. Hagar is an Egyptian-she is a Gentile, not of the chosen race of Abram.

The Lord shows Hagar mercy.

She is instructed to return to her mistress and submit to her.

vs 10-12 The angel informs Hagar that she will have a son and she was to name him Ishmael and he would live in hostility toward his brothers.

In this account we see that God cares about our:
    pain
    hopelessness
    helplessness

He comes with His:
    Presence
    provision
    promise
    You saw me before I was born.
    Every day of my life was recorded in your book.
    Every moment was laid out
    before a single day had passed. ***Psalm 139:16***

vs 15-16 Ishmael was the father of the Arabs and the ancestor of Mohammad, the founder of Islam.

Vocabulary

Sarai- means contentious

submit- to yield to the power, control, etc of others; give in

*Hagar-*means flight

*dealt harshly-*Hebrew anah means afflict, chasten, force and hurt.

*despised-*to look down on with contempt. To regard as worthless.

*Kadesh-*means sanctuary

*Bered-*means hailstorm[35]

Beer Lahai Roi- means Well of the Living One Who sees me. It was located between Kadesh and Bered.

Kadesh is located in the southwest Negev, and was later called Kadesh Barnea.

*Ishmael-*means God hears

Submission is a heart attitude.

Obedience is an act of the will.

SUMMARY

Abraham had waited 10 long years for the fulfillment of God's promise of a son. Now with Sarai's suggestion he decides to act on his own. He fails to seek God's will. Abraham at this point is not acting in faith, but in doubt.

Application

How do you respond to difficult situations? Do you get angry and hateful? What do your reactions show about the condition of your heart?

Getting ahead of God puts us in dangerous territory.

Sarah had no idea of how far reaching her actions would be. We never know what consequences our sin might have, or how many innocent people may be affected.

We need to wait for the Lord's timing.

> No eye has seen, no ear has heard, no mind has conceived what God has prepared for those who love Him. *1 Corinthians 2:9*

Day Five

Genesis 17 Covenant of Circumcision

1. How old is Abram at this point?

2. By what name does the Lord identify Himself?

3. What instructions does the Lord give to Abram?

4. What does the Lord say He will do?

5. What is Abram's reaction?

6. What does God change? see **vs 5,15**

7. a. What does the Lord instruct Abraham to do? **vs 9-13**
   b. Who were required to do this?
   c. When was this to be done?

8. What would be the consequences for one who does not do so? **vs 14**

9. a. What revelation did God give to Abraham about Sarai?

b. What was Abraham's response to this?

10. What did the Lord change?

11. Who would God establish His covenant with?

12. What promise does God give concerning Ishmael?

13. How old is Ishmael at this point?

14. When would Isaac be born?

15. a. What did Abraham do that very day?
    b. Who all was this done to?

16. How old is Abraham at this point?

17. Mark the words *covenant, circumcision*.

Correlation

A. *Circumcision-*
    1. What instructions are given concerning circumcision in **Leviticus 12:3?**

    2. Was circumcision meant as a guarantee for salvation?

See **Jeremiah 9:25; Romans 3:30**
    3. What does Paul say the purpose of circumcision is according to **Romans 4:11-12**?

    4. a. What does Paul say about circumcision in **1 Corinthians 7:19; Galatians 5:6; 6:15**?
        b. What is it that counts?

    5. What type of circumcision does Paul speak of in **Colossians 2:11**?

6. What does Paul say regarding circumcision in **Romans 2:25-29**?

7. What does **Jeremiah 4:4** instruct concerning circumcision?

B. Names
1. a. What are we told in **Revelation 2:17**?
   b. Who will receive this?

Outline

A. Renewal of the Covenant and a New Name for the Lord
B. God's Part of the Covenant
C. Sarah's Part of the Covenant
D. Abraham's Response
E. God's Promises for Ishmael.

Commentary

vs 1 Abram at this point is 99 years old. There is a thirteen year gap between this chapter and the last one during which the Lord apparently hasn't spoken to Abraham. All these years Abraham had believed that Ishmael was the fulfillment of God's promise. Why did God not speak to Abraham for thirteen years? God sometimes lets us struggle when we choose to do things our way. He does this to teach us to learn to trust and follow Him instead of leaning on our own understanding.[36]

This is the fifth appearance of God to Abram.

God here refers to Himself as El Shaddai-God Almighty, referring to His all-sufficiency.

Both Abraham and Sarah had yet to discover and trust the Lord as "God Almighty", the One who could override natural laws of reproduction. They had experienced God as Elohim-their shield, protector and provider. But they were unable to understand that God would fulfill His promise of a child in a supernatural way.³⁷

vs 5 Changing of a persons name signified a change in their character or destiny. All people involved in this event have their name changed. The Lord reveals Himself by a new name. Abram and Sarai both have the addition of an *"h"* to their names.

Every time Abraham heard his new name, he would be reminded of God's promise.³⁸

"I have made you" Notice this statement is given in present tense- signified that God's word was as good as done.

circumcision- the word means "cutting around", and symbolized belonging to a covenant people, the man would forever be identified as a Jew.

It was symbolic of:
    cutting off the old life of sin
    purifying one's heart
    wholehearted consecration and dedication of oneself to God.

vs 7 establish-means to set in motion. Notice that God is the one who initiated the relationship.

vs 10 This is the first mention of famine. How different from God's original provision in the garden.

vs 12-eight days old-why then? This is the the first day that the blood of a newborn is fully capable of clotting.

vs 14 cut off-disinherited and disowned.

vs 15 Sarah is the only woman in the Bible whose name is changed by God.

vs 16 God specifies that the son of promise will come from Sarah. He also names the child.

vs 17 Abraham responds by laughing-remember Sarah is 90 and Abraham himself is almost 100! Imagine the thought of caring for a baby at that age.

vs 18 Abraham appears to be attempting to get the Lord to accept Ishmael as the son of promise, or may be asking what was to be his destiny.

vs 20 God reassures Abraham about Ishmael-"I have heard you", and tells Abraham that Ishmael would be blessed and would be fruitful, and would father twelve rulers and would make him into a great nation.

vs 21 A specified time for the birth of the son is now given.

vs 23 Here we see Abraham's immediate obedience.

Vocabulary

blameless-hebrew-tamim does not mean to be perfect, but to be whole, entire, complete, spotless, having integrity.

We can only be complete when we are in fellowship with God.

God Almighty-El Shaddai-God of infinite power and sustenance, all sufficient.

fruitful-Hebrew parah "to bear fruit; bring forth fruit; to be, cause to be, make fruitful, grow or increase.

establish-**vs 7** means "to set in motion"

Abram-exalted father

Abraham-father of a multitude

Sarai-princess or contentious.

Isaac-he laughs

Food for Thought

Why was circumcision to be performed on the eighth day?

On the eighth day the infants immune system is at the optimum level for such a procedure. Important blood clotting agents, vitamin K and prothrombin are at their highest levels in infants on precidely the eighth day of life, making it the safest day to circumcise an infant.[39]

SUMMARY OF THE ABRAHAMIC COVENANT

A. Promises
   1. Many descendants **vs 4,6**
   2. Land **vs 8**
   3. Yahweh would be the God of Abraham and his descendants **vs 7-8**

B. Conditions of the Covenant
   1. Moral Uprightness
   2. Serve only Yahweh
   3. Circumcision of all males eight days old

C. Recipients of the Covenant
   1. Abraham and his descendants

D. Extent of the Covenant
   1. Everlasting

WEEK SIX

Day One

Genesis 18 Three Visitors

Looking at the Text

1. a. Who appeared to Abraham?
   b. Where was Abraham?

2. How did Abraham greet the men?

3. What hospitality did Abraham show these men?

4. What did the visitors ask Abraham? See **vs 9**

5. a. What did the Lord tell Abraham at this point?
   b. When would this occur?

6. a. What was Sarah's reaction to this statement?
   b. What are we told about Sarah in **vs11?**

7. What does the Lord say concerning Sarah's thought?

8. What does the Lord state about Abraham in **verse 18**?

9. What are we told is the reason the Lord chose him?

10. What does the Lord tell Abraham concerning Sodom and Gomorrah?

11. a. What is Abraham's reaction?

12. What does Abraham call the Lord in **verse 25**?

13. What is Abraham's attitude when he was speaking to the Lord?

14. How many did the Lord finally agree to spare the cities for?

Correlation

A. *Entertaining strangers*
   1. a. What are we told not to forget to do in Hebrews 13:2?
      b. Why are we to do this?

B. *Destruction of the wicked*
   2. What are we told concerning how God feels about destroying the wicked in the following verses?
      Ezekiel 18:23
      Jeremiah 18:7-8
      Jonah 3:10; 4:2
      2 Peter 3:9

C. *The Promise*
   3. Compare the promises given by the Lord to Abraham in these passages. How do they differ?
      Genesis 12:2-3
      Genesis 15:4-5; 13-16, 18-21
      Genesis 17:2,4-9,15-16; 19-21
      Genesis 18:10, 18

D. Abraham's Sons
   4. What is stated about Abraham's descendants in **Romans 9:7-9**?

E. Proper Prayer
   5. What are we told in **1 Timothy 2:1-4**

F. Intercessor
Abraham interceded for the cities of Sodom and Gomorrah.
   6. Who according to **Hebrews 7:25** is our intercessor?

Personal Application

vs 6 What situation are you facing that you feel is "too hard for the Lord"? What does this say about your view of God?

Outline

A. Abraham Visited by Three Men
B. Abraham Intercedes for Sodom

Commentary

vs 2-"bowed low to the ground" bowing conveyed an attitude of :
   reverence
   respect
   humility } toward another
   homage

vs 6-8 here we see Abraham's generous hospitality. He welcomes the strangers warmly and is not put out. He himself *runs* and selects a *choice, tender calf*. And he brings the food to them and stands nearby to bring them anything they may require.

vs 9 Notice that the visitors address Sarah by her new name. Only the Lord would know this.

vs 10 this is the sixth appearance to Abraham of the Lord. He again confirms His promise to not only Abraham, but this time Sarah as well. This must have happened shortly after the Lord had given Abraham the covenant of circumcision when the Lord told Abraham that Sarah would bear a child "by this time next year." **17:21**

We see here that the birth of Isaac had an "appointed time".

vs 12 Sarah had hoped for so long without results that she was probably afraid to hope again.

vs 13 The Lord knows everything about us. We can not hide anything from him.

Psalm 94:11 The Lord knows the thoughts of man; He knows that they are futile.

vs 14 God can do anything! Nothing is too hard for Him.

This event apparently happens shortly after the events of the last chapter.

The promise-notice that God continually encourages Abraham by reaffirming His covenant. The Lord starts out with general promises and each time He gives Abraham more specific information concerning the promise.

Example-"I will make thee a great nation", **Gen 12:2**. This would mean that Abraham would have descendants.
Abraham would be a father.

> "This shall not be thine heir, but a son coming from your own body" **Gen 15:4**

> "I will bless Sarai and give you a son by her" **Gen 17:16**

Your wife Sarah will bear you a son, and you will call him Isaac. I will establish my covenant with him as an everlasting covenant for his descendants after him. ***Gen 17:19***

But my covenant I will establish with Isaac, whom Sarah will bear to you by this time next year." ***Gen 17:21***

Abraham would have a son by his wife Sarah.

His name would be Isaac, and he would be born this time next year.

vs 19 keep-literally means "to hedge about with thorns"[40]

Abraham's Intercession

vs 20-33 "their sin is very grievous" Hebrew kabob-literally means "to be heavy".[41]

Notice that the Lord initiates the conversation, and He also concludes it.

Abraham intercedes with the Lord on behalf of Sodom and Gomorrah. His intercession was:
1. a request, not a demand. It was made with humility and respect.
2. Based on God's character and will.
3. Humble
4. earnest and fervent
5. persistent-he made six different petitions.[42]

vs 26 This is grace-sparing the wicked on behalf of the righteous.

Application

In this account Abraham gives us a good example of showing hospitality. Hospitality is a Greek word that means love of strangers.

In this account we see that it is not the presence of evil that brings God's mercy and patience to an end, but the absence of good.[43]

We also see the principle of intercessory prayer. Abraham interceded on behalf of others. He could have had a judgmental attitude that the city was wicked and deserved what they got for their wicked deeds.

Do you plead on behalf of others or do you wish they get punished? Do you practice hospitality?

Day Two

Genesis 19 The Destruction of Sodom and Gomorrah

Observation

1. Where was Lot sitting?

2. What did Lot insist the men do?

3. What did Lot serve his guests?

4. a. Who came to Lot's house?
   b. What did they want?

5. What did Lot offer them instead?

6. What was their response to this?

7. What did the angels do?

8. What instructions did the angels give to Lot?

9. What was the response of Lot's sons-in law?

10. What did Lot do when the angels told him to hurry and leave?

11. What did the angels do?

12. What four instructions did the angels give to Lot?

13. Where did Lot request to go?

14. When did Lot get there?

15. a. What did Lot's wife do?
    b. What happened to her?

16. Where did Lot and his two daughters go?

17. What did Lot's daughters do to their father?

18. What was the result?

Correlation

1. a. What are we told about Sodom and Gomorrah in **Jude 7**?
   b. What do they serve as an example of?

2. What does **Ezekiel 16:49** say that the sin of Sodom was?

3. What does Jesus say regarding Sodom in **Matthew 11:24**?

4. What does **2 Peter 2:6** say Sodom and Gomorrah served as an example of?

5. What does **Amos 3:6** tell us about when disaster falls upon a city?

6. What do we learn about the Lord in **Isaiah 31:2; Isaiah 45:7**?

7. What are we told about Lot in **2 Peter 2:7-8**?

8. What are we told in **Leviticus 18:6** regarding incest?

9. Compare Noah and Lot.

A. *Homosexuality*
1. What are we told in **Leviticus 18:22** regarding homosexuality?

2. What according to **Leviticus 20:13** was the penalty for engaging in homosexuality?

3. What are we told in **Romans 1:26-27**?

4. What are we told in **1 Corinthians 6:9-10** about who will not inherit the kingdom of heaven?

5. If a person is guilty of engaging in this sin, will they never be able to enter heaven? See **1 Corinthians 6:11**.

Outline

A. God Rescues Lot
B. God Destroys Sodom and Gomorrah
C. Lot and His Daughters

Commentary

vs 1 The fact that Lot was sitting in the gateway of the city indicates that he had become a man of prominence in the city. The city gate was where legal and business transactions were performed.

Lot lost all sense of moral values. He had grown up under the influence of Abraham, but chose to follow the world. In this account we see that a person is not so much a product of his environment as he is of his choices.

vs 8 What a despicable act for a father to do. He could have offered himself.

vs 11 These people were spiritually blind, and now they were physically blind.

vs 13 *destroy-* see **Genesis 6:13**

vs 14 Lot's daughters were pledged to be married, yet Lot was willing to offer his virgin daughters to the men of the city to "do what you like to them" see **vs 8**. Lot was as depraved as the men of Sodom were.

vs 16 *compassion, merciful-* Hebrew *chemiah-*only used here and in **Isaiah 63:9**. It refers to God's sparing His people, delivering them out of judgment because of His mercy. It can be translated "the merciful sparing of the Lord".

vs 18 Unlike his uncle who had interceded for others, Lot is concerned only about his own safety.

Lot's wife

We are never told what her name is. We know nothing about her. She was probably from Sodom.

vs 26 We aren't told why she looked back. She probably didn't want to leave her friends and possessions.

Few things are more dangerous than looking back to that from which God has delivered us.

Lot's daughters

We are never told what their names are.

Lot's daughters commit incest with their father after they get him drunk. They apparently brought the alcohol with them. They each get pregnant.

The oldest named her son Moab which means "from father".

The youngest had a son which she named Ben-Ammi which means "son of my people".

From them descended the Ammonites and Moabites, who became Israel's bitter enemies.

Vocabulary

Sodom-means place of lime *Gomorrah*-means submersion *Zoar*-small or little one.

SUMMARY

What a sorry statement on the city of Sodom that even 10 righteous people could not be found.

In this account we see God's:
>   judgment
>   grace
>   mercy
>   love
>   patience
>   righteousness

Christians are warned not to love the world.

> Love not the world, neither the things that are in the world. If any man love the world, the love of the Father is not in him. 16 For all that is in the world, the lust of the

flesh, and the lust of the eyes, and the pride of life, is not of the Father, but is of the world. *1 John 2:15-16*

Be not conformed to this world... *Romans 12:2*

Ye adulterers and adulteresses, know ye not that the friendship of the world is enmity with God? whosoever therefore will be a friend of the world is the enemy of God. *James 4:4*

We are told of God's coming judgment on the present corrupt world.

Lot vs Noah
1. Both were warned of impending judgment upon the wicked.
2. Both were righteous men. See **Genesis 6:9; 2 Peter 2:7.**
3. The families of both were included in God's salvation.
4. Unlike Noah, Lot was saved because the Lord "remembered Abraham". See **19:29.**

Lot's wrong choices.
1. He followed the path of friendship with the world.
   See **James 4:4**

2. He loved the world.
   See **1 John 2:15-16**

3. He conformed to the world.
   See **Romans 12:2**

4. Judgment with the world
   See 1 **Corinthians 11:32**

Sodom would have destroyed Lot if the Lord had not destroyed Sodom.

In wicked societies moral and ethical failures lead to social injustices.[44]

As Benajah Carroll states so well, "After every one of them was stricken blind, they groped for the door still to commit that sin. If you want a picture of the persistence of an evil passion, when the heart is hard and the neck stiffened, when the soul is incorrigible and obdurate, take the picture of these people blinded by the judgment of God and yet groping for the door."[45]

Day Three

Genesis 20 Abraham and Abimelech

Observation

1. a. Where did Abraham go?
   b. Where did he stay?

2. What did Abraham day about Sarah?

3. What happened?

4. a. What did God do?
   b. How did God communicate with him?
   c. Compare this with how he deals with Pharaoh in **Genesis 12:17**

5. What was Abimelech's response?

6. a. What does God tell Abimelech He knew?
   b. What did God do because of this?

7. a. What instructions does the Lord give to Abimelech?

b. What warning does the Lord give to Abimelech if he does not obey?

8. a. What does the Lord call Abraham?
   b. What does the Lord say Abraham would do?

9. a. What does Abimelech do the next morning?
   b. What is their reaction?

10. What three questions does Abimelech ask Abraham?

11. What three excuses does Abraham give for his actions?

12. a. What does Abimelech give to Abraham?
    b. Why does he do this?

13. What are we told that the Lord had done to Abimelech's household?

Correlation

1. What are we told in the following verses about what the Lord knows?
   1 Kings 8:39
   1 Chronicles 28:9
   Luke 16:15

2. What warnings are we given in the following verses?
   Galatians 6:7-8
   Numbers 32:23

Vocabulary

Gerar-located in southern border of Canaan.

*healed-rapha-*to cure, mend, repair, restore health

Abimelech-means "my father is king". It was a title not a name-like Pharaoh.

Commentary

Vs 1-2 Abraham left Mamre to go to Gerar after living in Mamre about 23 years. Why does he leave now? Perhaps because of the stench of burning sulfur-see **19:24**.

Gerar is the Philistine capital. It is located between Kadesh and Shur.This is apparently immediately after Sodom and Gomorrah's destruction.

Here again Abraham's fear causes him to take matters into his own hands. He sees things from his own viewpoint and focuses on the problem instead of on God. He either didn't learn his lesson the first time or he has forgotten. He repeats the same mistake he made in Egypt.

This is an example of what happens when we fail to trust God and depend on Him in all situations.

Did Sarah perhaps attempt to remind him?

Remember Sarah at this point is 90 years old, and yet is apparently very beautiful.

Abraham's actions threaten the promised son.

The Lord appears to Abimelech in a dream-once again communicating to a heathen. Abimelech pleads his innocence.

The Lord acknowledges his innocence, showing that the Lord knows the heart.

vs 7-first use of the word *prophet*-one who speaks for God

This is the first reference to *prayer*. This is an intercessory type prayer on the behalf of another.

vs 11 Abraham had acted out of fear instead of faith. David shows us how to respond to fear. He doesn't deny the feeling, but he chooses how he will respond to it. He doesn't let fear control him.

> When I am afraid, I will put my trust in You. **Psalm 56:3**

In his doubt, Abraham lies. Warren Wiersbe says "this damages his character because he loses his integrity. His testimony about God to his neighbors is severely damaged."[46] Non believers are watching how we live our lives. When we don't "walk the walk", it hurts our testimony. In this account the pagan Abimelech is more upstanding than God's own prophet. How sad. How many times are believers guilty of "living like the world"?

Abraham judged Abimelech, but Abimelech is seen to be more righteous than Abraham, who ends up being rebuked by the pagan.

Abraham's prejudices give a poor witness to the pagans.

Abraham acted out of fear. We all have vulnerable points. We must know what they are so that we can guard against making poor choices out of fear.

Application

We all have vulnerable points and fears. We need to be aware of them so we can guard against them. What are yours?

Genesis 21 The Birth of Isaac

1. What two things are we told here the Lord did for Sarah?

2. When was Isaac circumcised?

3. How old was Abraham when Isaac was born?

4. What happened during the feast of Isaac's weaning?

5. What was Sarah's reaction to this?

6. What was Abraham's reaction?

7. What did the Lord instruct Abraham to do?

8. What does Abraham do?

9. Who does Hagar encounter?

10. a. What are we told about Ishmael?
    b. Where did he live?
    c. What was his occupation?
    d. Where did he get a wife?

11. a. Who came to Abraham?
    b. What statement does the visitor make about Abraham?

12. What request does he make?

13. What complaint did Abraham have?

14. What was Abimelech's response?

15. a. What did Abraham give to Abimelech?
    b. What was the purpose of this?

16. What did Abraham do at Beersheba?

17. By what name does Abraham call God?

18. Where did Abraham stay?

Correlation

1. What does **Galatians 4:22-31** tell us concerning these two sons of Abraham?

Outline

A. The Birth of Abraham's Promised Son
B. Hagar and Ishmael Sent Away
C. Treaty at Beersheba

Commentary

vs 1 God is faithful and trustworthy. He keeps His promises.

The Lord waited until it was impossible for Sarah and Abraham to have children naturally, so that they would know beyond all doubt that it was God fulfilling His promise to them.

Ishmael is fourteen when Isaac is born.

vs 6 Isaac's name would remind Abraham and Sarah of their unbelief.

vs 8 Weaning-A feast was usually held when a child was weaned because it meant they would usually live to adulthood. The typical length of time a child was weaned was about 3 years of age.

vs 9 Mocking- **Galatians 4:29** says Ishmael *persecuted* Isaac.

vs 10 Drive out-expel Hebrew garash-same word used for expulsions of Adam and Cain after their sins.[47] See **3:24; 4:14**.

There is no record of Isaac and Ishmael seeing each other again until they bury Abraham.

vs 11-13 Abraham is distressed over what Sarah says. Remember that originally Sarah was the one who involved Hagar and Abraham heeded her then. See **Genesis 16:2.** The Lord reassures Abraham that He would make Ishmael into a nation, but instructs him to "do as Sarah says" and send Ishmael away. The Lord knows there would only be strife if he remained. Ishmael is probably about 17 years old at this point.

vs 14-Abraham doesn't delay in obeying, sending them off "early the next morning". He is apparently depending on God to care for them, because he sends them away with only a skin of water and some food. The Lord did promise that "the son of the bondwoman will I make a nation, because he is thy seed." **vs 13**

Wilderness of Beersheba- located 20 miles west of the southern end of the Dead Sea.

vs 16 Here we see Hagar in a state of utter despair and hoplessness. It appears as though she had forgotten about her earlier experience with the Lord.

vs 17 Notice that God hears "the boy crying"

The angel calls Hagar by name. He comes to Hagar-she doesn't call to God.

Here we see God's care and provision for the oppressed.

> For he shall deliver the needy when he crieth; the poor also, and him that hath no helper. 13 He shall spare the poor and needy, and shall save the souls of the needy. ***Psalm 72:12-13***
>
> He healeth the broken in heart, and bindeth up their wounds. ***Psalm 147:3***

vs 21 Wilderness of Paran-West of the Gulf of Aqaba in northern Sinai desert.

vs 32 Abraham is apparently living in Beersheba at this point. Gerar to Beersheba is 25 miles.

Abraham is visited by Abimelech. It has been about four years since their last encounter. Abraham's life has become a witness and testimony that "God was with him in everything he did."

Abraham again calls upon the Lord, calling Him the Eternal God, a reference to His eternal nature.

Vocabulary

Philcol-means mouth of all, or mouthful

mocking-Hebrew sahaq-to laugh out-right (in merriment or scorn); by implication to sport: laugh, mock, play, make sport. Same word used for caress in **Genesis 26:8**.

Beersheba-well of seven or well of oath. It is the southernmost point of the Promised Land.

It is the site of several encounters with God:

> Hagar-**Genesis 21:17**
>
> Isaac- **Genesis 26:23-33**
>
> Jacob-**Genesis 46:1-5**

SUMMARY

Warren Wiersbe tells us, "God's children grow in godliness and faith as they wait for the fulfillment of God's promises. Faith is a journey.[48]

Day Four

Genesis 22 Abraham's Test

Observation

1. What instruction does the Lord give to Abraham? **vs 2**

2. What does Abraham do? When does he do this? **vs 3**

3. How long was the journey? **vs 4**

4. What two things did Abraham tell his servants? **vs 5**

5. a. What does Isaac carry?
   b. What does Abraham carry? **vs 6**

6. What does Isaac ask his father? **vs 7**

7. What answer does Abraham give? **vs 8**

8. What three actions does Abraham perform here? **vs 9**

9. a. Who calls to Abraham?
   b. From where did he call? **vs 11,15**

10. What was Abraham's response?

11. What do we learn is the reason or purpose that God tested Abraham? **vs 12**

12. What happened next? **vs 13**

13. What name did Abraham give to the place? **vs 14**

14. a. What promise does the Lord make to Abraham?

      b.   Why does the Lord make these promises? **vs 15-18**

15. a.   Who was Abraham's brother?
      b.   Who was his brother's wife?

16. a.   How many sons did Abraham's brother have?
      b.   What were their names?

17. a.   Who was Abraham's brothers concubine?
      b.   How many sons did she have?

18. Who was Bethuel the father of?

Correlation

A. *The Lord Provides*
    1. What are we told the Lord provides in the following verses?
        2 Corinthians 9:10
        1 Thessalonians 1:7
        Philippians 4:19

B. *Abraham's Faith*
    1. a.   What are we told about Abraham in **James 2:21-23**?
        b.   How was Abraham's faith made complete?
        c.   What was Abraham called?

    2. a.   What does **James 2:17** say that faith should be accompanied by?
        b.   What does **James 2:20** say about faith that is not accompanied by this?

    3. What does **Hebrews 11:17-18** state about Abraham?

    4. What are we told in **Hebrews 11:19** that Abraham believed?

C. **Tests and Trials**
1. What are we told about temptation in **James 1:13**?

2. What is the progression of temptation as seen in **James 1:14-15**?

3. What are we told in **Psalm 66:10** that God does?

4. What are we told in **Isaiah 48:10**?

5. a. What do we learn about the purpose of trials in **1 Peter 1:6-7**?
   b. What is faith more precious than?

6. What does the testing of our faith develop according to **James 1:4**?

7. What will the person who perseveres under trial receive according to **James 1:12**?

D. **Sacrifices**
1. What are sacrifices that the Lord desires?
   Psalm 40:6
   1 Samuel 15:21
   Isaiah 1:11-17
   Psalm 82:3-4
   Hosea 6:6.

E. **Fear of the Lord**
1. What are we told in the following verses concerning the fear of the Lord?
   Proverbs 1:7
   Proverbs 9:10
   Job 28:28

F. *God's Faithfulness*
   1. What are we told in **Hebrews 6:13-15**?

   2. When according to **vs 15** did Abraham receive what was promised?

Application

vs 1 Is there something that God is asking you to give up, or sacrifice?

vs 14 What do you need the Lord to provide?

Day 5

Commentary

vs 1,11 Note that the Lord calls Abraham by name.

God tested Abraham… The devil tempts men in order to hurt them, but God tests men in order to strengthen them. James Baxter says "When the devil tempts it is that the tempted may fall; but when God tests it is that the tested may stand."[49] God does test our faith, but He does not tempt us and He cannot be tempted. God's purpose in testing a person is to confirm and strengthen, while Satan's purpose is to corrupt and weaken a person.

God wanted Abraham to sacrifice His own will and surrender it to God. He wanted to prove the validity-authenticity of Abraham's faith.

True worshippers acknowledge that everything belongs to God and will hold nothing back, trusting the Lord to provide for all your needs.[50]

Abraham responds to God's call "Here I am"-Hebrew henani-this is the attitude of a slave who desires to do his masters bidding. It conveys honor, respect, humility and loyalty. It is a desire to serve well.[51]

vs 2-3 Abraham apparently doesn't question or argue with the Lord. He doesn't put off or delay in obeying the Lord. Procrastination- putting off doing something difficult makes it harder.

Here we have the first use of the word ***love***.

vs 4 It was a three day journey. Imagine the heavy heart Abraham must have had. He had plenty of time to rationalize and come up with an excuse not to obey.

It was about 50-60 miles from Beersheba to Mount Moriah.

This is the very place where Christ Himself would be sacrificed.

vs 5 Notice what Abraham tells his servants here. ***We*** will worship, and ***we*** will return to you. This is the first use of the word *worship*.

Abraham didn't know what was going to happen, but he knew three things:
1. Isaac was to be the vehicle of God's promises, therefore Isaac must live.
2. God is trustworthy and always keeps His promises.
3. God's power was absolute even over the power of death.

Abraham therefore concluded that God would miraculously restore Isaac to life.

Oh too have that kind of faith!

vs 7 First use of the word ***lamb***.

vs 8 Abraham identified who would actually take Isaac's place. The **LAMB** would be provided by God and would BE God.

vs 9 This was Abraham's fifth altar. He had been building altars and worshipping God ever since God called him out of Ur. The previous altars were in response to God's promises. This altar was different. On it Abraham would sacrifice the fulfillment of God's promises to him.

Isaac had trust in his father. He was probably a teenager at this point. The word used for boy in **verse 5** is the same word used for Joseph in **Genesis 37:2** who was seventeen. Abraham was probably over 110 years old! So Isaac apparently allowed himself to be bound.

vs 11 God is never late.

We must always be sensitive to the Lord's voice. Imagine if Abraham had said to himself he must finish what he had started before he responded to God's call. God never intended for Abraham to sacrifice Isaac, but Abraham didn't know that.

vs 12 What does it mean "to fear the Lord?"
1. Reverence Him as sovereign.
2. Trust Him implicitly.
3. Obey Him fully and without protest.[52]

Abraham's willing obedience to God's instructions showed that God was the most important thing to Abraham. It reflected a heart willing to please God above anything, no matter what the cost to himself was. What are you putting above the Lord? To what or whom are you clinging? Only after you have placed your sacrifice on the altar will you be ready for God's provision.

Here God states three things about Abraham's actions:
1. "Now I know that you fear God" **vs 12** God knew all along, but did Abraham know to what degree he would obey God until he had been tested?
2. You have not withheld your son-your only son from Me **vs 12**
3. You have obeyed my voice **vs 18**

This defines the elements of worship:
1. Walking in fear-reverence of God
2. Full obedience to God's Word
3. Withholding nothing from God
4. Surrender to the Lord's will

vs 13 Recall Abraham's words to his son in **vs 8** And Abraham said, My son, God will provide himself a lamb for a burnt offering:

This is a picture of Christ's substitutionary atonement on our behalf.

> But he was wounded for our transgressions, he was bruised for our iniquities: the chastisement of our peace was upon him; and with his stripes we are healed. ***Isaiah 53:5***

vs 14 The Lord will provide! He is our provider as well. God didn't ask anything more of Abraham than what He Himself was willing to do. He provided His own Son as the perfect sacrifice for our sins, which provided our salvation.

vs 16-18 This is the Lord's seventh promise. The Lord swore by Himself because there was nothing greater to swear by.

Note the reason the Lord says He is making this promise-"because you have obeyed Me".

All nations on earth would be blessed through Abraham's offspring. This referred to Christ's victory over the enemy.

Here we see the first use of the word ***obey.***

vs 20-24 These verses tell about Abraham's brother Nahor and his wife Milcah. They had 8 sons. Nahor had a concubine named Reumah who also gave Nahor 4 sons. Nahor's son Bethuel had a daughter named Rebekah.

Food For Thought

The level of anxiety in your life can be connected to your sense of control. When we feel out of control, our anxiety levels rise.

The distance between a response of fear and one of exhilaration is the belief we have that the situation truly is under control, even if it is not our control... We may feel that we are free-falling through life, but we are held by God, who is in absolute control. Having faith that the situation is never out of God's control can calm our fears.[53]

Corrie ten Boom said that "Faith sees the invisible, believes the unbelievable, and receives the impossible."

Vocabulary

love-Hebrew ahab-to love, desire, delight.

worship-Hebrew shachah-fall down, bow down, fall prostrate. To regard with great honor, devotion, and respect. To attribute worth.

test- Hebrew nasah-idea of proving the quality of something, usually by putting it through some kind of trial; to attempt to learn the nature of something.

Mount Moriah-means "chosen by God." Located in Jerusalem. It was the place where the temple was eventually built-see **2 Chronicles 3:1**. Isaac died figuratively in the location where sacrifices were offered in preparation for Christ's coming. This was the same location where Christ was crucified.

SUMMARY

Put yourself in Abraham's place. How would you have responded?

God did not give Abraham this severe test until Abraham had been walking with God for many years. God leads us from "faith to faith" **Romans 1:17**.

Abraham's faith was not instant, but grew over time, as does ours. Abraham was saved by faith, but his faith was made evident through his obedience. His faith was expressed by his actions. He chose to obey.

Our pain and trials are not wasted. They are given or permitted to deepen and refine our character, perseverance, and faith.

God sometimes wants to demonstrate to us truth about His faithfulness, or about ourselves. Only through tests or trials do we move from theoretical to practical faith. Out responsibility is to obey and leave the details to God.

Amy Carmichael says faith is not "trusting God when we understand His ways"-there is no need for faith then. Faith is trusting when nothing is explained.[54]

Faith:
sees the invisible
believes the unbelievable
receives the impossible
Corrie ten boom

If we are always trying to live safely, we will never accomplish anything of lasting value.

I wonder if Isaac heard the angel call to Abraham? How do you think this may have affected Isaac's view and relationship with God? I find an interesting reference in **Genesis 31:53** when Jacob makes a treaty with his father-in-law Laban he "took an oath in the name of the Fear of his father Isaac."

Application

Is there something the Lord is asking you to "sacrifice"? A habit, a relationship?

Comparison of Isaac and Jesus

Both were the "only son" of their father Both trusted their father

Both were offered as sacrifices

Both carried the "wood" upon which they were to be sacrificed Neither resisted their own sacrifice

Journey to Moriah was three days. It was three days to the resurrection

Genesis 23 Death of Sarah
Observation

1. How old was Sarah when she died?

2. Where did she die?

3. a. Who did Abraham speak to?
   b. What does he state about himself?
   c. What does he request?

4. What title is Abraham referred to by? **vs 6**

5. What offer is made to Abraham?

6. What does Abraham do? **Vs 7**

7. a. What request does Abraham make?
   b. Of whom does he make this request?

8. How much does Abraham pay for Sarah's burial site?

9. Where was the burial site located?

Correlation

1. For more on Sarah, see the following verses:
   Isaiah 51:2
   Romans 4:19; 9:9
   Galatians 4:22-31
   Hebrews 11:11

Commentary

vs 1 Sarah is the only woman in the Bible whose age at death is recorded. Isaac is 37, and Abraham is 147 at this point.

vs 2 This is the first use of the word weep.

vs 3 Sons of Heth... Descendants of Heth became the Hittites. Heth was the grandson of Ham, one of Noah's sons. These people were a dominant force in Canaan from the time of Abraham to the twelfth century.

vs 4 This is the first reference in the Bible to a burial site.

vs 6 The Hitites recognize Abraham as a mighty prince, or "God's chosen one" HCSB. Abraham's life had been a witness to them.

vs 7 Abraham...bowed down. He showed respect to the men.

vs 9-11,16,18 This was a legal transaction which occurred at the city gate where legal and business transactions were conducted. It was witnessed by the Hittite elders.

vs 11 Abraham refused to accept this generous offer. He would not take anything from men. See **Genesis 14:22**.

vs 15 400 shekels of silver is equivalent to about 10 pounds.

vs 17 This verse specifically mentions trees. This may have been an additional value in the selling price.

The land Abraham purchases at this point is the only land which he ever owned in the Promised Land. The burial place is still in existence.

Abraham is 137 years old and Isaac is 37 years old at this time.

Hebron-This was where David ruled from for the first seven years of his reign.

SUMMARY

As does everyone, Sarah had her faults and her trials. She was faithful to Abraham. She is an example for women today.

> In the past, the holy woman who put their hope in God also beautified themselves in this way, submitting to their own husbands, just as Sarah obeyed Abraham, calling him lord. You have become her children when you do what is good and do not give way to fear. ***1 Peter 3:5-6***

WEEK SEVEN
Isaac

Day One

Genesis 24 A Wife for Isaac

Observation

1. What do we learn here about Abraham?

2. a. What request does Abraham make?
   b. Of whom does he make this request?

3. What concern does the servant have?

4. What encouragement does Abraham give?

5. What would free the servant from the oath?

6. a. How many camels does the servant take?
   b. What does the servant take with him?
   c. Where does the servant go?

7. What time of day is it?

8. What do we learn here about the servant?

9. What sign does the servant ask for?

10. a. What happens?
    b. When does this happen?

11. How is the girl described?

12. What request does the servant make?

13. What is the girl's response?

14. What did the servant give the girl?

15. What two questions does the servant ask the girl?

16. Whose daughter is she? (see also **vs 15**)

17. What does the servant do?

18. Who was the girl's brother?

19. How does the brother refer to Abraham's servant?

20. What would the servant not do until he tells of his mission?

21. How does the servant introduce himself? (**vs 34**)

22. What does the servant say about God in **vs 48**?

23. What does the servant ask in **vs 49**?

24. a. Who responds?
    b. What is their answer?

25. What is the servants response?

26. a. What did the servant give?
    b. To whom did he give these?

27. What did the servant say the next morning?

28. What is the response of her brother and mother?

29. What does the servant say?

30. What does Rebekah say?

31. Who does Rebekah's family send her away with?

32. Where was Isaac living?

33. What was Isaac doing when the party arrives?

34. What does Rebekah do?

35. Find all the references to the Lord in this narrative.

Correlation

A. Prayer
   1. What are we told concerning prayer in **Matthew 21:22**?
   2. What are we told in **James 1:6-7** about when we ask for something from God?

Outline

A. An Important Mission Given
B. Depending on God's Guidance
C. A Successful Mission

COMMENTARY

vs 1 Here we see that the Lord has kept His promise. He has blessed Abraham in every way. God is faithful to His word.

vs 2-eldest servant-the servant is never named, but may be Eliazar-see **Genesis 15:2**.

put your hand under my thigh-similar to today's handshake. The person who was taking the oath placed their hand in a very intimate place as a sign which expressed complete trustworthiness.

thigh-Hebrew yarek-be soft or of soft tissue.

vs 6,8 If the woman the servant chose was unwilling to come back with the servant, he was then free from his obligation. Under no circumstances was Isaac to leave the land of promise.

vs 10 Aram-naharaim-means Aram of the two rivers. Also called Paddan-Aram-Field of Aram.[55] See **Genesis 25:20**. This was Ur of Chaldees-See **Genesis 11:28,31; 15:7; Nehemiah 9:7; Acts 7:4**.

This was a trip of 450 miles one way. The servant took 10 camels which would carry the gifts for the bride price, and supplies for the trip.

vs 11 Not one word is said about the journey. We aren't told how long it took.

vs 12-14 The servant doesn't depend on his own judgement. He prays for God's guidance. He gives a sign for the Lord to indicate that the woman who fulfills this is the one which the Lord has chosen.

vs 15. The Lord answers the servant's prayer before he had even finished praying. Jesus told us that the Father knows our needseven before we ask Him.

> Your Father knows what you need before you ask Him. Prayer is essential for us to know and follow God's direction for our lives. ***Matthew 6:8***

God is always at work even if we are unaware of His actions.

vs 17-20 A camel can drink up to 25 gallons of water, and there are ten of them.

vs 24 Nahor is Abraham's brother. Rebekah is the daughter of Nahor's son Bethuel.

vs 26-27 The servant worships the Lord saying that the Lord had shown his master kindness and faithfulness.

vs 29-30 When he saw the earring and bracelets... Here we get a glimpse into Laban's character.

Rebekah's name means loop, or tie as in a tie rope for animals or a hitching place. When applied to a female it suggests her beauty by which men are snared and bound.[56]

vs 33-40 The servant refuses to eat until he relays his mission. He states:
1. Who he is-notice he doesn't give his name, only that he is the servant of Abraham.
2. wealth of his master
3. His mission-to find a wife for his master's son
4. Relays the Lord's guidance in his mission.

vs 50 Laban and Bethuel both realize that the events had been orchastrated by God.

vs 53- The gifts given are the bride price paid for Rebekah.

vs 54-55 Rebekah's family don't want her to leave immediately. They want her to stay ten days, but the servant is eager to return to his master.

vs 57 Rebekah is given the choice if she will go immediately, and she agrees to go immediately.

vs 62 Beer-lahai-roi-this is the well wher Hagar encountered the Angel of the Lord-see **Genesis 16:14.**

vs 63 Again we are told nothing of the journey.

vs 67 Isaac was comforted after his mother's death... We are told in **Genesis 25:20** that Isaac was 40 when he married. He was 37 when his mother died. It has been three years since her death.

SUMMARY

In this narrative, we are never told Rebekah's age. This narrative pictures the Trinity.

Abraham stands for God the Father

Isaac represents God the Son-awaiting His bride.

The servant represents the Holy Spirit whose mission is to call people to faith in the Lord, and win the bride for Christ.[57]

Word Wealth

Laban means white

meditate-suah means walk about, pray, lament, moan

Day Two

Genesis 25

Observation

A. Abraham's Death
 1. Who did Abraham take as a wife?

 2. a. How many children did she have with Abraham?
    b. What were their names?

3. Who were the sons of Jokshan?

4. Who were the sons of Dedan?

5. Who were the sons of Midian?

6. What did Abraham do with these sons?

7. How old was Abraham when he died?

8. a. Who buried him?
   b. Where was he buried?

9. Where did Isaac live?

B. Ishmael's Sons
   10. a. How many sons did Ishmael have?
       b. Name them

   11. How old was Ishmael when he died?

   12. a. Where did Ishmael's descendants settle?
       b. What are we told about them?

C. Isaac's Descendants'
   13. How old was Isaac when he married?

   14. Who did he marry?

   15. a. What problem did Isaac's wife have?
       b. What did Isaac do?

   16. What did Rebekah inquire of the Lord?

   17. What did the Lord tell her?

18. a. How old was Isaac when the twins were born?
    b. What were their names?
    c. What do their names mean?
    d. Who was the first-born?

19. What are we told about each son?

20. a. Whom did Rebekah favor?
    b. Whom did Isaac favor?
    c. Why did Isaac favor him?

21. a. What did Jacob sell to Esau?
    b. What did he sell it for?

22. What was Esau's view of his birthright?

Correlation

1. What are we told in **Romans 9:11-12** concerning the birth of Esau and Jacob?

2. What warning are we given in **Hebrews 12:16** concerning Esau's actions?

3. We see that Esau was ruled by his fleshly appetites. What warning are we given in **Philippians 3:18-19?**

Day Three

Outline

A. Death of Abraham
B. Ishmael's Descendants
C. Jacob's Sons

Commentary

A. Death of Abraham

vs 1 Here we are told that Abraham married a woman named Keturah. This was presumably after Sarah's death. We are not told anything at all about her-her age, her ancestry, or her death. We only know that Abraham married her and she bore him six sons. We are told that one of the sons-Jokshan had two sons-Sheba and Dedan and that Dedan was the father of Asshurim, and Letushim, and Leummim. These were the descendants of the Asshurites, Letushites, and Leummites.

Another son Midian had five sons. He was the descendant of the Midianites which were a nomadic tribe that settled in the desert area southeast of Canaan.

vs 5 Abraham left everything he owned to Isaac. He gave gifts to his other sons and sent them east.

vs7-9 Abraham lived to be 175 years old-38 years after the death of Sarah. He was "full of years" meaning he had lived a full life. He was buried by his sons Ishmael and Isaac. We don't know how Ishmael learned of Abraham's death. Perhaps Abraham sought him after Sarah's death. Ishmael is 89 years old and Isaac is 75 years old at this point. Isaac's sons Esau and Jacob are 15 at this point. See **Gen 25:26**.

Isaac had married when Abraham was 140 years old. Esau and Jacob were born when Abraham was 160 years old. (See **Genesis 25:20,26**)

vs 11 Isaac was living at Beer-lahairoi at this time.

vs 12 We are not told who Ishmael married.

SUMMARY OF ABRAHAM'S LIFE

1. What characteristics did Abraham's life reveal?
2. Which of these characteristics do you see in your own life?

Abraham's life was one of faithfulness, obedience and trust.

His life can be summed up in that He believed the Lord.

> And he (Abraham) believed in the Lord and it was credited to him as righteousness. ***Genesis 15:6***

He is an example of what James tells us.

> What doth it profit, my brethren, though a man say he hath faith, and have not works? can faith save him? 17 Even so faith, if it hath not works, is dead, being alone. ***James 2:14, 17***

When Abraham willingly obeyed the Lord to sacrifice Isaac, he proved his faith in God through his actions, as well as proving that he loved God more than the gift he had received from God. Genuine faith results in heartfelt obedience. Our works don't save us but they are proof of our salvation.

Abraham was chosen by God. God initiated the relationship. Abraham wasn't seeking after God. God chose him not because of his own merit, but because of God's grace. God calls us into a relationship that requires:

> Look to Abraham your father and to Sarah that bore you: for I called him alone, and blessed him, and increased him. *Isaiah 51:2*
> faith- **Genesis 12; Hebrews 11**
> worship-evidenced by the altars Abraham built
> obedience-**Genesis 12**
> submission-**Genesis 22**
> action-Abraham left Ur, and was circumcised
> waiting-Abraham waited 25 years for the birth of his son

Is God calling you? In our materialistic society the loud voice of consumerism can often drown out God's "still small voice" (**1 Kings 19:12**) Is His voice being drowned out? Or are you simply unwilling to respond? Are you being hard hearted?

> ... today if ye hear His voice, harden not your hearts. *Hebrews 4:7*

There were several incidents in his life which show us the danger of going our own way instead of following God. When Abraham went to Egypt and Gerar he went his own way. He also chose to do things his own way when he had Ishmael.

He received the covenant of circumcision. We are told in **Romans 4:11-12** that circumcision was a sign that Abraham already had faith and that God had already accepted him and declared him to be righteous—even before he was circumcised. So Abraham is the spiritual father of those who have faith but have not been circumcised. They are counted as righteous because of their faith.

> And he received the sign of circumcision, a seal of the righteousness of the faith which he had yet being uncircumcised: that he might be the father of all them that believe, though they be not circumcised; that righteousness might be imputed unto them also: 12 and the father of circumcision to them who are not of the circumcision only, but who also walk in the steps of

that faith of our father Abraham, which he had being yet uncircumcised. ***Romans 4:11-12***

Abraham was known as "the friend of God" See **2 Chronicles 20:7; 41:8; and James 2:23**. Abraham didn't call himself God's friend, God called him that. What would God say about you? Remember that the Lord had revealed to Abraham his plans about Sodom and Gomorrah.

Through Abraham God had promised to bless "all peoples on earth through you". This was fulfilled through his descendant Jesus Christ who was the promised Messiah.

Abraham had faith in three areas:
1. Faith to Risk-He left all to follow God's call.

2. Faith to believe God would do as He promised.

3. Faith to surrender-was willing to give God full obedience no matter what the cost.[58]

God revealed Himself to Abraham as:
  Yahweh-the Lord
  El Elyon-God Most High
  El Shaddai-God Almighty, the all sufficient One
  Yahweh Jireh-Lord our provider

He was a man whose life was marked by building altars and calling on the name of the Lord. See **Genesis 12:7; 13:4,18; 22:9**

The Lord spoke with Abraham on eight different occasions. See **12:1-3, 7; 13:14-17; 15:1- 21; 17:1-22; 18:1-33; 21:12-13; 22:1-2,11-18**

Although Abraham was a man of faith, his faith wasn't perfect. He was an ordinary man with flaws, like everyone.

Lessons which Abraham learned and we also learn:

1. God calls us to righteousness, not based on our own righteous acts which are like filthy rags-see **Isaiah 64:6,** but on our faith. See **Genesis 15:6; Romans 4:3**

2. It is dangerous to take matters into our own hands. See **Genesis 16**

3. God still loves us and can and will still use us even when we detour from His plan, if we return to His path. See **Genesis 12:10-19; Genesis 16**

4. We must wait for God's perfect timing. **Genesis 18:10**

5. God can do what for man would be impossible. Nothing is too hard for God. **Genesis 18:14; Jeremiah 32:17.**

6. God is trustworthy-He keeps His promises **Genesis 21:1-7.**

7. Blessings ultimately follow obedience. **Genesis 22:18**.

8. He is the example of what it means to live a life of faith. Even though in his lifetime he never saw the fulfillment of God's promise, he kept his focus on God and not on what he had left behind.

    These all died in faith, not having received the promises, but having seen them afar off, and were persuaded of them, and embraced them, and confessed that they were strangers and pilgrims on the earth. 14 For they that say such things declare plainly that they seek a country. 15 And truly, if they had been mindful of that country from whence they came out, they might have had opportunity to have returned. *Hebrews 11:13-15*

9. We too are sojourners in this world. This world is not our home.

> For this world is not our permanent home; we are looking forward to a home yet to come. *Hebrews 13:14*

His life is summarized in **Hebrews 11:8-12**

> By faith Abraham, when he was called to go out into a place which he should after receive for an inheritance, obeyed; and he went out, not knowing whither he went. 9 By faith he sojourned in the land of promise, as in a strange country, dwelling in tabernacles with Isaac and Jacob, the heirs with him of the same promise: 10 for he looked for a city which hath foundations, whose builder and maker is God. 11 Through faith also Sara herself received strength to conceive seed, and was delivered of a child when she was past age, because she judged him faithful who had promised. 12 Therefore sprang there even of one, and him as good as dead, so many as the stars of the sky in multitude, and as the sand which is by the seashore innumeral.

We are children of Abraham if we are believers in Christ.

> And if ye be Christ's, then are ye Abraham's seed, and heirs according to the promise. *Galatians 3:29*

Abraham's Travels

11:31 Ur of Chaldees

12:4 Haran

12:6 Tree of Moreh at Shechem

12:8 Hills east of Bethel-pitched tent with Bethel on west and Ai on east

12:9 Abraham continued toward Negev **12:10** Abraham went down to Egypt **13:1** Went back to Negev

13:3 Back east of Bethel

13:18 Trees of Mamre at Hebron

20:1 Region of Negev and lived between Kadesh and Shur

For a while stayed in Gerar

22:19 Beersheba

23:2 Kiriath Arba-Hebron

IMPORTANT EVENTS IN LIFE OF ABRAHAM

75-Called by God to leave his home and go "to the land I will show you". **Gen 12:1**

86-His son Ishmael is born **Genesis 16:16**

99-God appears to Abraham and changes Abram and Sarai's names. He gives Abraham the covenant of circumcision. Promise of Isaac is given. **Genesis 17**

100-Isaac is born **Genesis 21:5**

112?-Abraham offers Isaac as a sacrifice. **Genesis 22**

137-Sarah dies **Genesis 23:1**

140-Isaac marries Rebekah **Genesis 25:20**

160-Esau and Jacob born **Genesis 25:26**

175-Abraham dies **Genesis 25:7-8**

B.   *Ishmael's Death and Descendants*

vs 12-18 Ishmael became the father of twelve sons. This fulfilled the Lord's promise in **Genesis 17:20**. We aren't told who his wife was. In **Genesis 21:21** we are told that his mother got him a wife from Egypt.

His sons lived in an area from Havilah to Shur toward Asshur. Havilah is a region in north-central Arabia. Shur is between Beersheba and Egypt. It is between modern day Suez Canal and Wadi el Arish.[59]

Ishmael died at the age of 137.

C.   *Jacob and Esau*

vs 20 Isaac was 40 years old when he married. Abraham was 140 at this point.

vs 21 Rebekah like her mother-in-law Sarah was barren. Isaac prayed for his wife. Isaac would have realized what God could do since he himself was the result of God's miraculous provision. He unlike his parents responded in faith instead of taking matters into their own hands. This was a time of testing for Isaac. How do you think Abraham may have felt during these years of waiting?

vs 21-26 Rebekah becomes pregnant with twins. We don't know her age. Jacob was 60 at this time, and Abraham was 160 at this time. The name Jacob comes from Hebrew yaaqob which means "may God protect". It sounds like aqeb which means heel, and aqab which means "watch from behind", or overtake.[60]

The struggle that began in the womb would continue throughout their lives and down through the generations.

vs 27 Esau is a skilled hunter, a man of the outdoors. Jacob was a quiet man, who stayed at home.

vs 28 Family strife is caused by favoritism. Here we see a dysfunctional family. Isaac loved Esau, Rebekah loved Jacob.

vs 29-34 Here we see a little more into the character of the twins. Esau was impatient and controlled by a fleshly appetite. He placed more value on satisfying his physical appetites than he did on achieving spiritual blessings. Jacob was shrewd and calculating.

When we are weary we are more vulnerable to temptation.

Vocabulary

birthright-right of the firstborn son to receive a double portion of the inheritance and became head of the family.

despised-bazah-to disesteem.

Application

Have you ever been so focused on a physical desire that it consumed you and caused you to have poor judgment?

Do you value earthly things more than eternal treasures and blessings?

Jesus instructed us in **Matthew 6:33** Seek first His kingdom and His righteousness and all these things (material needs) will be given to you.

We are told in **Luke 12:34** Where your treasure is, there your heart will be also.

Day Four

Genesis 26 Wandering and Digging Wells

1. What problem does Isaac face?
2. What did Isaac do?
3. a. What instructions does the Lord give to Isaac?
   b. What promises does the Lord make to Isaac?
   c. What reason does the Lord give for making these promises to Isaac?
4. a. What deception does Isaac use?
   b. What happens?
5. What are we told about crops Isaac plants?
6. a. What do the Philistines do?
   b. Why do they do this? (**vs14**)
7. What does Abimelech tell Isaac?
8. What does Isaac do?
9. a. What confrontation does Isaac become involved in?
   b. What were the names given to the wells dug by Isaac's servants, and what were the meaning of the names?
10. a. Where did Isaac move to? (**vs 23**)
    b. What happened there?
11. What promise does God make when He appears to Isaac again?
12. What does Isaac do after this encounter with the Lord?
13. a. Who came to visit Isaac?
    b. What was the purpose of the visit?
    c. Compare this encounter with the earlier one involving Abraham-see **Genesis 21:22-33**
14. What was Isaac's response to them?
15. What was the outcome of the encounter?
16. What did Isaac do after this?
17. a. How old is Esau when he married?
    b. Who did he marry?
    c. What is the reaction of Isaac and Rebekah?

OUTLINE

I. Isaac in Gerar
II. Wandering and digging wells
III. Isaac and Abimelech
IV. Esau's Marriage

Vocabulary

Beersheba-well of oath or well of seven.

Sitnah-opposition

Commentary

vs 1 This is the first promise from the Lord to Isaac.

vs 7 Isaac prejudges out of fear. God had just spoken to him and promised to be with him and yet Isaac still takes matters into his own hands.

Esau and Jacob are adults at this time. If Isaac and Rebekah had children with them, it would have been apparent they were husband and wife. See **vs 34**. We don't know where Esau and Jacob are living at this time.

vs 10 Here we see the pagans acting with more integrity than Isaac. Isaac's actions are a poor witness.

vs 14 This is the first use of the word *envied*. God's blessings can lead others to become jealous of us.

vs 17-22 Digging wells. Isaac apparently learned to keep peace from his father.

vs 24 Here the Lord appears again to Isaac and and again renews the covenant which He had made with Abraham.

vs 25 Here is the first altar built by Isaac.

vs 26 Isaac is visited by Abimelech.

vs 28 Abimelech states that it was clear the Lord was with Isaac.

vs 29-31 The two parties share a meal and make a treaty of peace.

vs 34-35 Esau's marriage. He was the same age as his father Isaac had been when he married. See **Genesis 25:20**.

Word Wealth

vs 8-*caressing* Hebrew sahaq-to laugh outright (in merriment or scorn); by implication to sport: laugh, mock, play, make sport. Same word for mocking found in **Genesis 21:9**.

Application

vs 19-22 How do you react when you have been wronged?

Matthew 5:9 Blessed are the peacemakers, for they will be called sons of God.

Day 5

Genesis 27 Deceiving and Scheming

Observation

1. What do we learn in **vs 1** about Isaac?

2. Who did Isaac call to him?

3. What does Isaac tell this person?

4. Who overheard the conversation?

5. What does Rebekah tell Jacob to do?

6. What is Jacob's concern?

7. What is Rebekah's response?

8. a. List Isaac's suspicions. **vs 19-27**
   b. List the times Jacob lies.

9. What was the blessing that Isaac gave?

10. How does Isaac react when he realizes what has happened?

11. What does Esau say about Jacob?

12. What blessing does Isaac give to Esau?

13. a. What does Esau plan to do?
    b. When does he plan to do this?

14. a. Who is told what Esau plans to do?
    b. What does this person do?

15. Where does Laban live?

16. What does Rebekah complain to Isaac about?

Food For Thought

1. What were Rebekah's motives for her actions? Were they purely selfish, or was she trying to see that God's prophecy would come to pass?

2. What might have been a better way to deal with the situation?

3. What do Rebekah's actions reveal about her relationship with Isaac?

Correlation

1. What are we told in **Hebrews 11:20**?

2. What are we told in **Malachi 1:2-3** about Jacob and Esau?

3. What does **Romans 9:10-13** tell us about why God had chosen Jacob?

A. *Lying*
4. What according to the following verses is the Lord's attitude about lying?
   Proverbs 6:17
   Proverbs 12:22

5. What instructions are we given in **2 Corinthians 4:2**?
6. What instructions are we given in **Ephesians 4:25**?
7. What are we told in **Galatians 6:7**?

B. *Vengeance*
8. According to the following verses, to whom does vengeance belong?
   Proverbs 24:29
   1 Peter 2:21-23

9. What instructions are we given in **1 Thessalonians 5:15**?

C. *Anger*
10. What are we told in **Ephesians 4:26**?

Outline

A. Passing on the Birthright
B. Deception
C. Deception Discovered
D. Jacob Flees to Haran

Commentary

vs 1-5 Isaac plans to give his blessing to his favorite son Esau. Isaac at this point is over 100 years old. Isaac was 60 when Jacob and Esau were born, and Esau was 40 when he married. See **Genesis 25:26; 26:34.**

vs 5-10 Rebekah's actions here show a lack of faith in the Lord's promise. She felt that she needed to help God, reminding us of Sarah. We are not sure if her motives were to see her favorite receive the blessing, or if she was trying to fulfill the Lord's revelation she received when she was pregnant.

In these events we see that Rebekah has a manipulative nature.

vs 7 Rebekah emphasizes the fact that the blessing will be given in the Lord's presence. This may indicate she is attempting to fulfill the revelation she had been given.

vs 19 Here Jacob lies outright.

vs 24 Isaac is suspicious.

vs 27 Here is the first use of the word kiss. It was a kiss of deception. Judas gave Jesus a kiss of betrayal.

vs 33 Isaac's reaction when he realizes he had been deceived. He realized it was God's will.

vs 36,41 Esau said that Jacob "took my birthright". Esau knowingly and willingly sold his birthright. It was not taken from him. Here we see Esau's bitterness and failure to face his own lack of character.

vs 41 NIV grudge-first use of the word in Scripture. Esau plots to kill his brother, just as Cain had killed his brother. Actions taken by Esau:
> begged-**vs 34,38**
> cried- **vs 38**
> held a grudge-**vs 41**
> premeditated murder-**vs 42**
> consoled himself-**vs 42**

Characteristics we find in Esau are:
> bitterness
> selfishness
> failure to accept responsibility for his actions-he blames Jacob for stealing his birthright when he sold it of his own free will.
> revenge
> hatred
> anger

vs 42 Rebekah is told about Esau's plan, not Isaac.

vs 43-46 Rebekah comes up with another plot to save Jacob from Esau's plot. Note in **vs 45** her statement "forgets what you did to him". It wasn't Jacob's idea. He did it at his mother's urging.

Application

1. How do you react when you have been wronged? Do you seek revenge, or do you forgive the person who has wronged you?

SUMMARY

Actions have consequences, so we need to think before we act.

Consequences of Jacob and Rebekah's actions:
1. They never saw each other again
2. His brother wanted to kill him.
3. He was in exile from his family for twenty years.

Relationships between family members-spouses, parents, and children must be founded on the principles of truthfulness and honesty

WEEK EIGHT
Jacob

Day 1

Chapter 28 Fleeing

Observation

1. What does Isaac tell Jacob to do?

2. What does Isaac's blessing consist of?

3. What does Esau do when he saw that the Canaanite women did not please his father?

4. How is Bethuel referred to here?

5. a. Who does Jacob encounter on his trip?
   b. How does he identify himself?
   c. What promises does he make?

6. What is Jacob's response to this encounter?

7. a. What does Jacob name the place?
   b. What was the original name of the place?
   c. What does the name Jacob gave mean?

8. a. What vow does Jacob make?
   b. What was Jacob's focus?

Correlation

1. What are we told concerning Jacob's journey in **Deuteronomy 32:9-12**?

A. *Angels*
2. What are we told in **Hebrews 1:14** concerning angels?
3. What does Jesus say in **John 1:51**?

B. *Vows*
4. What are we told in the following verses concerning vows made?
   Numbers 30:2
   Deuteronomy 23:21
   Psalm 50:14
   Psalm 66:13-14
   Ecclesiastes 5:4-6
   Matthew 5:33

5. What do we learn from the account given in **Acts 5:1-11** about how seriously the Lord takes vows?

Observation

vs 5 Isaac is living in Beersheba-**Genesis 26:23**

Beersheba to Haran is a trip of about 400 miles. This would be a long, dangerous trip for a lone person.

vs 12-15 This is Jacob's first encounter with the Lord.

angels-God's messengers.

stairway-this is the only use of this word in all of Scripture.

In this encounter, the Lord renews His covenant with Jacob.

This is a revelation to Jacob that God was with him. It is an encouragement to what must have been a frightening time for Jacob. He is alone and traveling into an unknown situation.

The Lord promises to:
- guard
- guide
- protect
- provide

vs 18 Pouring oil was and act of sanctification and dedication. Jacob probably set up a monument instead of making an altar because he didn't have an animal to sacrifice.

vs 19 Luz was about 50 miles from Beersheba.

vs 20-22 Jacob's response is to give a conditional prayer. It seems as if Jacob is bargaining with God-"if you...then I" His relationship with God is new and He hasn't yet learned from experience that the Lord was trustworthy. In his prayer Jacob seeks the Lord's:
- promise
- presence
- protection
- provision

Jacob is still focused on the physicl and not the spiritual. He is self-centered. At this point he isn't necessarily concerned with what God wants, but with what God can do for him.

Jacob has had a personal encounter with the Lord, and his life will be changed by the encounter.

Application

1. Are you aware that God is in this place? God is always with us. Jesus promised to always be with us.

And surely I am with you always, to the very end of the age. *Matthew 28:20b*

Day 2

Genesis 29 Love at First Sight

Observation

1. Where did Jacob come to?

2. a. What did Jacob see?
   b. What were near it?
   c. What was covering it?

3. What questions does Jacob ask?

4. What does Jacob tell them to do?

5. What reason do they give for not being able to do this?

6. Who now comes on the scene?

7. What does Jacob do?

8. After he does this, what does he do?

9. a. What does Laban do when Rachel told him about Jacob?
   b. How does Laban greet Jacob? see **vs 13-14**

10. a. How long does Jacob stay with Laban? **vs 14**
    b. What does Laban tell Jacob at this point?

11. a. How many daughters did Laban have?
    b. What were their names?
    c. Who was the older one?

12. What are we told about each one?

13. a. Who was Jacob in love with?
    b. What proposal did he make?

14. What does Jacob tell Laban after he had fulfilled his time?

15. What does Laban do?

16. What did Laban give as a wedding gift?

17. What three questions does Jacob ask after he realized what had been done to him?

18. What is Laban's reason for his actions?

19. What does Jacob agree to?

20. What gift does Laban give Rachel?

21. What do we learn in **vs 30**?

22. What does the Lord see?

23. What are we told about Rachel?

24. a. How many children did Leah have?
    b. What were their names?
    c. What does Leah say after each birth?
    d. What is revealed about Leah from the names she gives her children and the statements she makes?

Outline

A. Love at First Sight-**vs 1-20**
B. What Goes Around Comes Around-**vs 21-28**
C. Leah's Struggle-**vs 30-35**

Correlation

A. *Reaping and Sowing*
   1. What warning are we given in **Galatians 6:7**?

B. *Marriage*
   1. What are we told in **Proverbs 30:21,23**?
   2. What law is given in **Leviticus 18:18**?

Commentary

vs 1 Jacob arrives in Haran. We aren't told anything more about his journey or how long it took.

vs 2,8-10 This may have been the same well where Eliezer met Jacob's mother Rachel. Rachel watered Eliezer's camels, and Jacob watered Rachel's sheep.

vs 11 Pent up anxiety and relief that the journey was finally over may have been one reason for Jacob's display of emotion here. A kiss was a sign of respect, affection, reverence or subjection.[61]

This is the only place in Scripture where a man kisses a woman who is not his wife of mother.

vs 18 Jacob agrees to serve Laban for seven years in return for his daughter Rachel as his wife.

vs 23-25 Jacob the deceiver is himself deceived. Just as he had used clothing to deceive his father, he also was deceived with the use of clothing-a bride would have been heavily veiled. God sometimes uses other people to discipline His children. God is not mocked-a person reaps what he sows.

Apparently Laban was the one behind the deception but the daughters would have had to have been participants as well. I can't imagine why Rachel would not have warned Jacob.

We are told that Jacob loved Rachel, but we are never told that Rachel loved Jacob. I would love to know more about how this was played out.

vs 31-35 In these verses we see Leah's struggle to be loved by her husband. She was a desperate woman who was devoted to her husband even though he didn't love her. She strongly desired his love, as is seen by her statements after the birth of her children:

vs 32 ...now my husband will love me.

vs 33...The Lord heard I was unloved...

vs 34...Surely this time my husband will feel affection for me.

By her fourth son she has apparently realized that her consolation would be found in the Lord alone

vs 35 This time I will praise the Lord.

Here we again see that the Lord is aware of when we are mistreated by others. He sees that Leah is unloved and honors her with children while keeping Rachel from conceiving. She gives birth in these verses to four sons.

Vocabulary

vs 17 *weak*-Hebrew rak-can mean gentle, tender, delicate, responsive. *Leah*-impatient, wild cow or weary.

Rachel-ewe

Laban-white

Reuban-see a son

Simeon- one who hears

Levi-attached or a joining

Judah-praise

SUMMARY

God was using the events in Jacob's life to transform him and humble him. Life's experiences should lead to self-examination so we can be sure that we are in God's will and following His directions.

Day 3

Genesis 30 Building Family and Fortunes

Observation

1.   a. What demand does Rachel make here?
   b. Who does she blame?
   c. What impression do you get of Rachel from this?

2.   a. What is Jacob's response?
   b. Who does he say is responsible?

3. What solution does Rachel decide on?

4.   a. How many children does Bilhah have?
   b. What names does Rachel give them?
   c. What statements does Rachel make about their births?

d. What do these statements reveal about Rachel's character?

5. What does Leah do when she realizes she has stopped bearing children?

6. a. How many children does Zilpah bear?
   b. What does Leah name them?
   c. What statements does she make concerning their births?
   d. What do these statements reveal about Leah?

7. a. What does Reuben find?
   b. When does he find these?
   c. What does he do with them?

8. What request does Rachel make of Leah?

9. What is Leah's response?

10. What offer does Rachel make?

11. a. Who listened to Leah?
    b. What does He do?

12. a. What does Leah name her fifth son?
    b. What does she say?

13. a. What does Leah name her sixth son?
    b. What does she say?
    c. What does this reveal about her desire?

14. What does Leah name her daughter?

15. a. Who remembered Rachel?
    b. What two actions does He take?

16. a. What name does Rachel give her son?
    b. What statement does she make?
    c. What does this reveal about her?

17. What does Jacob request of Laban after the birth of Joseph?

18. a. What does Laban say he has learned?
    b. How had he learned this?
    c. What does this reveal about Laban?

19. What does Laban tell Jacob to do?

20. What does Jacob tell Laban?

21. What did Jacob request for his wages?

22. a. What did Laban do that very day?
    b. In whose care did he put them?
    c. How far did he take them?

23. What did Jacob do when the flocks were in mating season?

Correlation

A. *Divination*
   1. a. What prohibition is given in **Leviticus 19:26,31**?
      b. Why was it prohibited?

   2. What does **Leviticus 20:6** say the Lord would do to a person who turned to mediums and spiritists?

   3. What does **Deuteronomy 18:9-13** instruct us?

Commentary

vs 1-4 Notice that neither Jacob or Rachel appear to pray to the Lord about Rachel's barrenness. Rachel, like Sarah takes matters into her own hands.

vs 5-8 Rachel's handmaid Bihah has two sons-Dan and Naphtali. She feels she is incompetition with her sister. She is barren, bitter and broken.

vs 9-13 Leah then in desperation gives her handmaid Zilpah to Jacob. who then has two sons-Gad and Asher.

Gad is the name of a god of fortune.[62]

Ashur is the name of a god of luck.[63]

vs 14-16 We see in these verses that Rachel lacks faith in God, trusting in mandrakes instead.

Mandrakes were a plant whose roots resembled the lower part of a human body and were believed to have properties that helped with conception.

Poor Jacob. Poor Leah. Leah tells Jacob that she has "hired him" and that he "must sleep with her". How sad!

vs 20 Leah was still trying to win the affection of her husband.

vs 22 Apparently Rachel at some point turns to the Lord, because we are told "He listened to her." As we saw with Abraham and Sarah delay does not necessarily mean denial with the Lord. It is in His time not ours.

vs 23 God had taken away Rachel's disgrace and added to her blessings.

vs 27 This indicated that Laban is a pagan. In **chapter 31** we will learn he also possessed household gods.

If I have found favor...How would he have found favor-by tricking him and forcing seven more years of servitude?

vs 37-42 Instead of trusting God to give him prosperity Jacob again schemes to try to get the better of Laban. He probably feels vindicated to do so because of Laban's cheating him out of seven years.

SUMMARY

Genesis 29-30 These two chapters cover a period of 20 years. In this dysfunctional family we see favortism, jealousy, competition and lack of trust.

Vocabulary

Dan-he has vindicated

Naphtali-my struggle

Gad-good fortune or a troop

Ashur-happy

Issachar-reward

Zebulun-honor

Dinah-judged or avenged

vs 22-*taken away*-Hebrew qsaf

too add-Hebrew yasef

Joseph-"may he add" or "the Lord increases".

Day 4

Genesis 31 Jacob Flees Laban

Observation

1. What do Laban's sons accuse Jacob of?

2. What does Jacob notice?

3. a. What does the Lord tell Jacob to do?
   b. What promise does the Lord make?

4. What does Jacob tell Rachel and Leah in **vs 5**?

5. What does Jacob say about:
   himself
   Laban
   the Lord

6. What did the Lord tell Jacob in a dream? **vs 12**

7. How does the Lord identify Himself?

8. What did the Lord tell Jacob to do?

9. What does Rachel and Leah say about their father?

10. What do they tell Jacob to do?

11. a. What does Rachel do?
    b. When does she do this?

12. Does Jacob tell Laban he is leaving?

13. Where does Jacob head?

14. When does Laban learn that Jacob had fled?

15. a. What does he do?
    b. Who does he take with him?

16. How long does it take for him to catch up with Jacob?

17. a. Who came to Laban in a dream?
    b. What warning is Laban given?

18. What three questions does Laban ask Jacob?

19. What does Laban accuse Jacob of?

20. What answer does Jacob give for leaving secretly?

21. What did Jacob declare about anyone who possessed Laban's gods?

22. What had Rachel done with the gods?

23. What does Rachel tell her father?

24. What is Jacob's attitude at this point?

25. What three questions does he ask of Laban?

26. How long had Jacob been in Paddan Aram?

27. What does Jacob state about his working conditions in **vs 38-41**?

28. a. What did Jacob say Laban would have done?
    b. What did Jacob say the Lord had done to Laban?

29. a. What does Jacob state about God?
    b. What three names does Jacob address God by?

30. What does Laban suggest they do?

31. What did they do to signify their covenant?

32. a. What name did Jacob call it?
    b. What did Laban name it?

33. What other two names was it given?

34. Who did Laban say was a witness between them?

35. What promise did the two parties make?

36. What did Jacob do at the site?

37. What names does Laban address the Lord by?

38. What name did Jacob take an oath in?

39. What does Laban do before he left to return home?

Correaltion

A. *Crying Out to the Lord*
   1. What does the Lord do when we cry out to Him? See **Psalm 120:1; 138:3**.

Outline

A. Jealousy
B. Jacob Flees Again
C. Pursued
D. Covenant Made

Commentary

vs 1 Blessings from God can often cause jealousy from others. We don't know how many sons Laban had.

vs 3 Lord's third appearance to Jacob.

vs 4-9 Jacob pleads his case to his wives.

He gives God the credit for protecting him from Laban's attempts to cheat him.

vs 10-13 The Lord's second appearance to Jacob.

We again see that the Lord sees when we are treated unjustly.

vs 14-16 Notice the anger that Laban's daughters feel toward their father.

vs 19 Rachel may have done this as an act of revenge, or she may not yet have been a true believer in the Lord. Nuzi tablets from the 15th century B.C. indicate that possession of these household gods would make the person the chief heir.

vs 20 Jacob is still a deceiver. He is again fleeing. But unlike when he fled fron Esau, this time he was not guilty of anything.

vs 21 Gilead- east of the Jordan River north of what is Jordan today.

vs 31 Fear often keeps us from trusting God. God wants us to trust Him in difficult circumstances because they may provide unusual opportunities that allow Him to demonstrate His care and concern.

vs 34 Rachel deceives her father as Jacob had deceived his father.

vs 36 Jacob is angry and defends himself.

vs 45-50 This treaty was the result of distrust between the two parties. They called on God to be a witness between them.

vs 55 This is the last mention of Laban.

Day 5

Genesis 32 Jacob Prepares to Meet Esau

Observation

1. Who met Jacob on his journey when he left Laban?

2. a. What does Jacob name the place of his encounter?
   b. What does this name mean?

3. Where did Esau live?

4. What do messengers tell Jacob concerning Esau?

5. a. How does Jacob react to this information?
   b. What action does Jacob take?
   c. What is the purpose of his actions?

6. What does Jacob do in **vs 9**?

7. What does Jacob remind the Lord of in **vs 12**?

8. What does Jacob send to his brother as a gift?

9. What did Jacob instruct his servants to say to Esau?

10. What was Jacob's purpose in sending the gifts?

11. Where did Jacob send his wives, maidservants and eleven sons?

12. What happened to Jacob during the night?

13. What was the result of this encounter?

14. a. What new name does Jacob receive?
    b. Why did he receive this name?
    c. What does this name mean?

15. a. What name does Jacob give the place of his encounter?
    b. What does this name mean?

Correlation

1. What are we told about this incident in **Hosea 12:3-4**?

Outline

A. Preparing to Meet Esau
B. Wrestling With God

Commentary

vs 1 Here we see how gracious God is by sending angels to give Jacob encouragement.

vs 3-5 Jacob sends messengers ahead to greet Esau. They return with the terrifying news that Esau has 400 men with him.

vs 7-8 Jacob divides his people into two camps.

vs 9-12 Jacob's prayer. In this prayer he:
1. Acknowledges God as the God of Abraham and Isaac.
2. States that he is obeying God's instructions.
3. Humbles himself before God-"I am unworthy"

4. Acknowledges that
5. 6. Reminds God of His promise.

vs 13-21 Jacob is probably where the saying "God helps those who help themselves" comes from. Jacob prays, but then takes matters into his own hands in an attempt to appease Esau with a gift.

What should we do when we face difficult circumstances? Seek God's wisdom so that we will continue to walk in God's will.

vs 24-29 Jacob's fourth encounter with the Lord.

During this encounter Jacob receives a new name.

Jacob's life had been based on self sufficiency. Here the Lord "cripples" his self-sufficiency so Jacob would have to rely on the Lord with greater faith and dependancy.[64]

It is not until the point that we are humbled that God blesses us.

Wrestlig with God-Jacob had spent his whole life struggling to gain God's blessing in his own strength. God would grant His blessing when and to whom He wanted. We cannot force Him to bless us.

It was not Jacob's cleverness or human strength that gave him victory but God's grace. The angel did not give in to Jacob's human strength, but dislocated his hip. We cannot encounter God without it affecting and changing us.

By seeking God's blessing and being weakened and forced to yield, Jacob had become a "prince with God".[65]

Peniel-means face of God

Israel-means he struggles, or God will rule, prince with God or may God preserve.

vs 31 Jacob was broken to be healed and weakened to be strengthened. Jacob's limp would be a constant reminder that God was in control of his life.[66] It is the same with us.

When we are weak we are strong in Christ if we depend on Him and not on ourselves

> And he said unto me, My grace is sufficient for thee: for my strength is made perfect in weakness. Most gladly therefore will I rather glory in my infirmities, that the power of Christ may rest upon me. 10Therefore I take pleasure in infirmities, in reproaches, in necessities, in persecutions, in distresses for Christ's sake: for when I am weak, then am I strong. *2 Corinthians 12:9-10.*

> For ye see your calling, brethren, how that not many wise men after the flesh, not many mighty, not many noble, are called: 27 but God hath chosen the foolish things of the world to confound the wise; and God hath chosen the weak things of the world to confound the things which are mighty; 28 and base things of the world, and things which are despised, hath God chosen, yea, and things which are not, to bring to nought things that are: 29 that no flesh should glory in his presence. God can only use us when we are willing to surrender ourselves to Him. *1 Corinthians 1:26-29*

Application

Are you so self sufficient that God has to "injure" you to break your self-dependence?

WEEK NINE

Day 1

Genesis 33 Jacob Reunited With Esau

Observation

1. What order did Jacob arrange his family to meet Jacob?

2. What did Jacob do as he approached Esau?

3. What five things did Esau do in his greeting of Jacob?

4. What does Jacob acknowledge in **vs 11**?

5. Where did Jacob tell Esau he was headed to?

6. a. Where did Jacob go?
   b. What did he build there?

7. a. What did Jacob purchase?
   b. Who did he purchase it from?
   c. What was the price he paid?

8. a. What did Jacob set up?
   b. What did he name it?
   c. What does this name mean?

Commentary

vs 3 bowing conveyed an attitude of:
    respect
    reverence }toward another
    humility
    homage

vs 4 Note Esau's greeting-He:
    runs to meet him
    embraced him
    throws his arms around his neck
    kissed him
    wept

vs 5,8 Jacob refers to himself as "your servant" and Esau as "my lord" indicating a humble position of servitude.

vs 6-7 Note the order of Jacob's family-from least important first to most important last, farthest from potential danger so if the meeting didn't go well Rachel and Joseph might have a chance to get away.

vs 19 This is only the second piece of land owned by Abraham and his descendants in the land that God had promised to Abraham. The first was the cave and field purchased by Abraham as a burial place. See **Genesis 23:17-18**.

Jacob sets up an alter to the Lord. This is a witness to the local inhabitants.

vs 20 This is the first altar built by Jacob. It was a witness to the pagans living in the land. The name means mighty is the God of Israel.

Application

Who do you need to be reconciled with?

Genesis 34 The Rape of Dinah
Observation

1. What did Dinah do?

2. Who was the ruler of the area?

3. What three actions did Shechem take?

4. What are we told in **vs 3**?

5. What did Shechem tell his father?

6. What was Jacob's reaction when he heard what had happened to his daughter?

7. What did Shechem's father do?

8. a. Where were Jacob's sons?
   b. What did they do when they heard what had happened to their sister?
   c. What was their emotional state?

9. What proposition does Hamor make?

10. What does Shechem say?

11. What are we told in **vs 13**?

12. What condition did Jacob's sons make?

13. What four things would Jacob's sons do if they did this? **vs 16**

14. What are we told about Shechem in **vs 19**?

15. What were the alterior motives of Hamor according to **vs 23?**

16. What was the response of the men of the city?

17. a. What happened three days later?
    b. Who did this?

18. Where was Dinah during this time?

19. What was Jacob's response to his sons actions?

20. List the actions of each character in the narrative:
    Dinah
    Hamor
    Shechem
    Simeon and Levi
    other sons of Jacob
    Jacob

Correlation

A. Rape
   1. What was the consequence of being found to not be a virgin when a woman married according to **Deuteronomy 22:13,20-21**?

   2. What were the laws concerning the rape of a betrothed woman when the rape occurred in:
      a. a city-see **Deuteronomy 22:23-24**
      b. in a field-see **Deuteronomy 22:25-27**

   3. What was the law concerning the rape of an unbetrothed woman according to **Deuteronomy 22:28-29?**

Read **2 Samuel 13:6-23,28,32**
1. a. Who was raped?
   b. By whom?

2. What are we told is the reaction of the victim?

3. What advice does her brother give her?

4. a. What does her brother do?
   b. When does he do this? see **vs 23**

B. *Vengeance*
1. a. What do the following verses say concerning vengeance?
   b. To whom does vengeance belong?
   Psalm 94:1
   Isaiah 34:5
   Romans 12:19

Commentary

vs 1 We aren't told why Dinah went to visit the women of Shechem, but she probably wanted some female company-she had twelve brothers.

vs 2 Did Shechem rape her or seduce her.

vs 5 I can't understand how a father could not react to his daughter being defiled.

vs 6 It seems Dinah's brothers are more grieved over this than her own father.

vs 13 Note that Jacob's sons reply deceitfully-like father like son.

vs 14 Circumcision was a symbol-it did not automatically mean that the one who was circumcised was in covenant with God. Only a commitment from a person's heart would do this.

vs 23 It appears there was an ulterior motive for the treaty on the part of the Shechemites.

Day 2

Genesis 35

1. a. Where did God instruct Jacob to go?
   b. What did God tell Jacob to do there?

2. What preparations did Jacob tell his family to do before they left on their journey?

3. What did Jacob say about God?

4. What happened to the towns around Jacob?

5. a. Who died in Bethel?
   b. What was the place where she was buried named?
   c. What does the name mean?

6. a. Who appeared to Jacob?
   b. What promises did he make?
   c. By what name does the Lord refer to Himself?

7. a. What is another name for Bethel?
   b. What is the significance of Bethel?
   c. What did Jacob do there?
   d. What did he call it?

8. Where did Jacob head for next?

9. What happened while they were traveling there?

10. a. What name did Rachel give her child?
    b. What did Jacob name the child?

11. Where did Jacob move next?

12. What did Reuben do?

13. Where did Jacob move to then?

14. a. How old was Isaac when he died?
    b. Who buried him?

Outline

A. Rededication
B. Death of Deborah
C. Death of Rachel
D. Death of Isaac

Commentary

vs 1 This was Jacob's fifth encounter with God.

vs 2 Jacob prepares his family by having them:
  get rid of their foreign gods
  purify themselves
  change their clothes

vs 4 Jacob buried the foreign gods under the oak at Shechem.

vs 6 This was the place where the Lord first appeared to Jacob-see **28:19**.

vs 8 When Rebekah's nurse Deborah joined Jacob we aren't told. It is interesting that her death is recorded in Scripture, but Rebekah's death is not recorded. She was buried under an oak, that was called Allon-bachuth which means "oak of weeping".

vs 9-13 This is the Lord's sixth appearance to Jacob. At this point the Lord restates the covenant promises. He reveals Himself to Jacob as El Shaddai-God Almighty.

vs 16-18 Here Rachel dies while giving birth to a son. Earlier she had said she would die if she didn't have children-see **30:1**. We don't know how old she is.

Rachel gives the child the name Ben-Oni meaning son of my trouble. Jacob renames him Benjamin meaning son of my right hand.

vs 21 Jacob moves from Ephrath to Migdal Edar.

vs 22 We are told that Reuben slept with Jacob's concubine Bilhah. Again Jacob shows passivity by not reacting when he hears about it. This was a sign of disrespect.

vs 27 Jacob moved to his father Isaac's home in Mamre near Kiriath Arba-Hebron.

vs28- 29 Isaac dies at 180 years of age. He is buried by his sons Jacob and Esau. Jacob and Esau are now 120 years old-they were born when Isaac was 60-see **Genesis 25:26**.

This is the last record of Jacob and Esau seeing each other.

Summary of the Character of Isaac

He had a yielding, passive disposition-**Genesis 22; 26:16-25**

He was contemplative-**Genesis 24:63**

Like his father, he lies to the people of Gerar about the fact that Rebekah is really his wife-**Genesis 26:12-14**

SUMMARY OF ISAAC'S LIFE

Events of Isaac's Life
age 3? Expulsion of his half-brother
teens Offered by his father on altar
37 His mother Rebekah dies
40 Marries Rachel
60 Birth of Esau and Jacob 180 Dies
He was promised by God (**Gen 18**)
He was mocked by Ishmael (**Gen 21**)
He was sacrificed by Abraham (**Gen 22**)
His bride was chosen by Eleazar (**Gen 24**)
He was confronted by the King of Gerar (**26:9-10**)
He was requested to make a treaty with Abimelech (**26: 26-29**)
He was deceived by Rebekah and Jacob (**27:1-29**)
Although Isaac was a passive person, there were two actions which He took himself:
1. He prayed for his wife (**Gen 25:21**)
2. He blessed Jacob (**Gen 28:1**)

Genesis 36 Esau's Descendants
Observation

1. How many wives did Esau have?

2. How many sons did Esau have?

3. Where did Esau settle?

4. How many sons did Seir the Hittite have?

5. What did Anah discover?

6. What did Hadad son of Bedad do?

Commentary

vs 3 Here we are given the names of two of Ishmael's daughters.

vs6-7 This sounds similar to Abraham and Lot.

vs 20-29 Descendants of Seir the Horite.

vs 31-39 Kings of Edom

vs 40-43 Chiefs descended from Esau.

Sidebar

Herod the Great, the man who murdered the Bethlehem children (**Matthew 2:16-18**) and his son Herod Antipas the one before whom Jesus was tried, were both Edomites, men from Idumea.[67]

Day 3

Genesis 37 Joseph and His Brothers

Observation

1. Where was Jacob living?

2. What are we told about Joseph?

3. a. What did Jacob do?
   b. Why did he do this?

4. a. What was Joseph's brothers attitude toward him?
   b. What were three reasons for their attitude? see **vs2-4, 8**

5. a. What did Joseph relate to his brothers and father?
   b. What was the response of Joseph's brothers?
   c. What was his father's reaction?

6. What errand did Jacob send Joseph on?

7. What did Joseph's brothers want to do to Joseph?

8. What does Reuben do?

9. What do Joseph's brothers do with him?

10. What do the brothers do after this?

11. What does Judah suggest they do with Joseph?

12. a. What price do they sell Joseph for?
    b. Who do they sell him to?

Correlation

1. What are we told in **Acts 7:9** about this incident?

A. *Instructions for Fathers*
   2. What instructions for fathers are found in **Ephesians 6:4; Colossians 3:21?**

B. *Hatred of Brothers*
   3. What are we told concerning hating our brothers in the following passages?
      1 John 2:9-11
      1 John 3:15
      1 John 4:20-21

C. Restoration of Relationships
4. According to **Matthew 18:15-17** what way should the brothers have handled the situation?

Outline

A. Joseph's Bad Report
B. Joseph Favored by Jacob
    a. Coat of many colors
C. Brothers Jealousy
D. Joseph's dreams
E. Joseph Sold by His Brothers

Commentary

vs 2 Joseph brings a "bad report" concerning his half-brothers. We don't know what they had done. This could be looked at as being a tattle-tale, but I think that even at this age Joseph had a high regard for right and wrong.

vs 3 Jacob was 91 when Joseph was born. He favors Joseph and he doesn't even try to hide it. He learned favoritism from his parents. Here we have another dysfunctional family.

vs 4 Here we see the terrible effects that favoritism has on other siblings. It causes resentment and hatred toward the one who is favored.

vs 6-7 Whether this was said with pride and arrogance or just an attempt to share an intriguing dream is unclear. He is a 17 year old teenager whose interpersonal skills may not have been well developed yet. Considering his apparent relationship with his brothers, it was poor judgment and naive to share this dream. The brother's hatred of him may have caused them to react to the dream with a mean spirit.

vs 8 Joseph's brothers hate him more now because of his words and dreams.

vs 12-17 Shechem was 50 miles from Hebron (Mamre). Dothan was 15 miles farther. This was a great distance to travel alone.

vs 20 Simeon and Levi have proven they have no qualms about murder-**Gen 24.**

vs 21 Reuben was the firstborn and would have traditionally received the double inheritance that was usually bestowed on the firstborn, so he had the most to loose. Yet we see here that Reuben attempts to rescue Joseph. He didn't agree with what his brothers were doing, but he apparently didn't have the integrity or courage to stand up to them.

vs 26 Judah suggests selling Joseph to the Ishmaelites. They were coming from Gilead headed to Egypt. There was a balm of Gilead which they may have been bringing for trade. See **Jeremiah 8:22; 46:11**.

vs 28-32 Joseph is stripped of his robe and sold for silver, just like Jesus was. The tunic was the symbol of their father's favor. Perhaps the brothers also desired to inflict pain upon the father who had shown such blatant favoritism.

Jacob who had deceived his own father using clothing, is now deceived by his own sons. Joseph's brothers were guilty of sinning against their brother and their father.

Joseph was sold for the price of a slave. See **Leviticus 27:5**.

We aren't told here of Joseph's reaction. We are told in **Genesis 42:21-22**. Imagine the fear and terror he must have experienced.

vs 29 Where did Reuben go? Perhaps he was on duty with the sheep.

Application

When have you failed to take a proper stand against a wrong being committed? What excuse did you give? "It's not my place or my business".

Vocabulary

vs 7,9-10 *bowed, bowing, bow*-Hebrew shachah-meaning to prostrate oneself[68]

vs 8 *reign*-Hebrew malak-means to ascend the throne[68]

vs 8 *rule*-Hebrew mashal-to reign, govern[68]

vs 10 *rebuked*-ga'ar-to chide[68]

Day 4

Genesis 38 Judah and Tamar

Observation

1. Where does Judah go?

2. What does Judah do while he is there?

3. How many sons does Judah have?

4. Where was his third son born?

5. Who did Judah get as a wife for his firstborn son?

6. What happened to Judah's firstborn son?

7. What did Judah tell Onan to do?

8. a. What did Onan do?
   b. What did the Lord do in response to Onan's actions?

9. a. What action does Tamar take?
   b. Why does she do this?
   c. What is the result?

10. What is Judah's reaction when he finds out that Tamar is pregnant?

11. What does he do when he is confronted by Tamar?

Correlation

1. Judah's lineage is seen in **1 Chronicles 2:3-4**.

A. *Leverite Marriage*
   2. What provision was made if a man died without a son as an heir? See **Deuteronomy 25:5-10**

B. *Passing Judgment*
   3. What are we told regarding passing judgment in **2 Corinthians 10:12**?

Commentary

vs 1 Adullam was a town southwest of Jerusalem near Bethlehem.

vs 2-5 Judah marries a Canaanite woman whose father was named Shua. She has three sons, Er, Onan, and Shelah who was born at Kezib.

vs 6 Judah gets a wife for Er named Tamar.

vs 7 Er is put to death by the Lord because he is wicked in the Lord's sight.

vs 8-10 Judah tells Onan to produce offspring for his brother. Onan doesn't do so, and this displeases the Lord, and he also is put to death by the Lord.

vs 11 Judah refuses to give his last son to Tamar. Tamar stays with her father.

vs 12 Judah's wife dies. He goes with his friend Hirah to Timnah where the sheep are being sheared. Note-Timnah is the city where Samson also took a Canaanite wife. See **Judges 14:1-2**

vs 13-14 Tamar's plot.

vs 20 The pledge Judah had given was more valuable than a goat. He sends his friend with the payment instead of going himself. Perhaps he was concerned about his reputation.

vs 21 NIV says "the road at Enaim". Enaim means two springs.

vs 24 Judah is told that his daughter-in-law Tamar is pregnant as a result of prostitution. Judah is quick to pass judgment on Tamar without even checking the facts.

vs 25-26 When Judah is presented with proof of the fact that he is the father, he admits that she was more righteous than he had been.

vs 29-30 Tamar has twins. Tamar is an ancestor of David-see **Ruth 4:18-21** She and her son Parez are in the genealogy of Jesus. See **Matthew 1:3; Luke 3:33.**

The scarlet thread tied to Parez's hand at birth symbolizes the "scarlet thread of redemption" that runs through the Bible. It depicts the blood of Christ and His royalty. The theme begins with the blood that was shed when God made coats to clothe Adam and Eve in the garden and continues to the cross where the Lamb of God was slain for sin.

Vocabulary

Tamar-date tree or palm tree

Er-watcher or watchful

Onan-strength or vigorous

Shelah-drawn out

Perez-bursting forth, breaking out or one who breaks through

Zerah-Drawing, shining, scarlet or brightness

Day 5

Genesis 39 Joseph and Pontiphar's Wife

Observation

1. a. Where was Joseph taken?
   b. How do you think Joseph might feel at this point?

2. What are we told in **vs 2** about Joseph?

3. a. What did Joseph's master realize?
   b. What did Pontiphar do because of this?
   c. What was the result of this?

4. What are we told in **vs 6** about Joseph?

5. What did Pontiphar's wife want from Joseph?

6. a. What is Joseph's response?
   b. What two reasons does Joseph give for his response?

7. What does Pontiphar's wife do?

8. a. What does Joseph do when he is cornered?
   b. What does he leave behind?

9. What does Pontiphar's wife do?

10. What is Pontiphar's reaction??

11. How do you think Joseph felt at this point?

12. What are we told about Joseph in **vs 21**?

Correlation

A. *Witnesses*
   1. Compare Joseph's witness for the Lord in **vs 9** with Abraham's witness in **Gen 12:17- 19**.

B. *Seduction*
   2. What are we told in **Proverbs 1:10**?

C. *Temptation*
   3. What promise is given in **James 1:12** regarding temptation?

   4. What do the following verses warn us to flee from?
   1 Corinthians 6:18
   1 Corinthians 10:14
   1 Timothy 6:9-11

   5. What are we told in **1 Timothy 6:11** we are to pursue?

   6. What are we instructed to do in **Proverbs 1:10**?

D. *Responding to Trials*
   7. a. How are we instructed to respond to trials in **1 Peter 4:12-13, 19**?

   8. What are we told in **1 Peter 3:14** about suffering for doing right?

   9. What encouragement are we given in **Romans 8:28**?

E. *Fornication*
   10. What did Jesus tell us about sexual sin in **Matthew 5:27-28**?

F. *God's Sovereignty*
   11. What does the Lord state that He does in **Isaiah 45:7**?

   12. What are we told in the following verses about who is ultimately in control of situations?
   Daniel 4:34-35
   Proverbs 16:33
   Lamentations 3:37-38

Commentary

vs 1 Pontiphar-captain of the guard

vs 2 The Lord was with Joseph...Joseph is prosperous and successful.

vs 3 Joseph's master realizes that the Lord is with Joseph.

vs 4 Pontiphar puts Joseph in charge of everything he owns.

vs 5 The Lord blesses Pontiphar because of Joseph. Remember that God had told Abraham that He would "bless those who bless you"; and that Abraham would "be a blessing". This promise was passed down through his offspring.

vs 6 We learn here that Joseph is well built and handsome. We will see that good looks can be a curse.

vs 7-9 We don't know how long Joseph has been in Egypt at this point. Here we see into Joseph's character. He is still somewhat arrogant-"No one in this house is greater than I." His response shows that he is a man of integrity. He gives a good testimony. His motivation was his devotion to God. Some people maintain a moral standard simply because they know what they could lose. They fear the shame and loss of reputation. Joseph had no family or friends. He was a slave in a foreign country and would have little to lose. It is our love for God that will keep us from falling into sexual sin. "How can I sin against God?" This is the level of devotion God wants from every Christian. This should be our attitude toward temptation.

Servants, be obedient to them that are your masters according to the flesh, with fear and trembling, in singleness of your heart, as unto Christ; 6 not with eyeservice, as menpleasers; but as the servants of Christ, doing the will of God from the heart; 7 with good will doing service, as to the Lord, and not to men: ***Ephesians 6:5-7***

> We are in the greatest danger of failing when everything seems to be going our way. Then we have no place to go but down. That is when we really need to be on guard.

> Whoever thinks he stands must be careful not to fall. ***1 Corinthians 10:12***

vs 10 She spoke to Joseph day after day... She is one persistent woman. Satan is also persistent in tempting us. He wants to wear us down. We must persevere.

Joseph avoided temptation by refusing to be around it.

Make not provision for the flesh, to fulfill the lusts thereof. If we know we are weak in an area, don't put yourself in that situation. ***Romans 13:14***

Compare Joseph's actions with Judah's.

vs 11 We need to avoid private places where temptations or false accusations can arise.

vs 13-19 Pontiphar's wife blames Pontiphar for her sinful actions. That is the way of the world, to blame others and not acknowledge when we have sinned. This is the second time that Joseph's clothes were used against him. Joseph is falsely accused and imprisoned. We aren't told Joseph's reaction.

Victor Hugo said "Hell hath no fury like a woman scorned."

vs 20 Attempted rape was a capital offense. The mild punishment which Joseph receives suggests that Pontiphar did not believe his wife. The King's prison was a place for political prisoners and would not be where foreign slaves would be put. But to protect his dignity, his marriage and his wife's reputation Pontiphar had to punish Joseph. Pontiphar was captain of the guard-see **39:1**. He would have been responsible for prisoners in this prison. So Joseph was in effect demoted.[69]

vs 21 The Lord was with Joseph...This fact resulted in:

> The prison warden show showing Joseph favor
>
> Joseph to have success in whatever he did
>
> Joseph being put in charge of the prisoners
>
> What then are we to say about these things? If God is for us, who can be against us? **Romans 8:31**
>
> Our job is to look for evidence of God's presence. When we focus on God's sovereignty in our lives we will see Him at work in our lives and we will be encouraged-even in the darkest hours.[70]

Vocabulary

Pontiphar-devoted to the sun

SUMMARY

God is sovereign and Joseph is where God wants Him to be. Jacob had shown Joseph favoritism. God had to remove Joseph from that situation. What in your life must be removed before God can use you as His instrument? Perhaps God needs to change an attitude or something about your personality needs to be dealt with. Maybe you are self- reliant or proud of an achievement or an accomplishment. Joseph needed some tweaking in his personality. God knew the best means of preparing him for his future assignment. This is a period of preparation for Joseph. He is learning skills he will later need to run the country.

God put Joseph in different situations where Joseph could only depend on God

>His brothers betrayed him.

>His owners wife lied about him.

Joseph had nowhere to turn but to God. God never betrayed him. On the contrary, **39:2,21** "God was with Joseph" God never abandoned Joseph and He will never abandon us. Has God put you in a situation that you have nowhere to turn but to God? He may be testing your faith or showing you that He is dependable and trustworthy.

God allowed Joseph to be in situations where he was absolutely helpless. Only God could rescue him. He did this so that Joseph would learn to depend on God.

Living an upright godly life does not mean that people will acknowledge that you are godly. Many times it leads to their being jealous and they attempt to cause you to sin.

Suffering is not always the result of sin in our lives. Another example of this is seen in Job.

Before we can exercise authority we need to learn how to be under authority.

Every trial is designed to reveal something about ourselves which we didn't know. It can reveal a strength or a weakness. They can strengthen our faith as we witness God's faithfulness.

Suffering is one of God's tools which He uses to gain our attention. C.S. Lewis said "Pain insists on being attended to. God whispers to us in our pleasures, speaks in our conscience, but shouts in our pain: it is His megaphone to rouse a deaf world."[71]

During this time Joseph was also a witness to Pontiphar and those around him.

Joseph apparently didn't feel sorry for himself. He did not let his circumstances dictate his response to them. As Matt Carter and Halim Suh state in their book Creation Restored The Gospel According to Genesis "Joseph's perception of reality didn't shape his beliefs. His beliefs shaped his perception of reality."[72] He could have become angry and resentful and lived in self-pity, blaming others for his problems, and fantitsizing about vengeance, wanting to get even with those who had wronged him. Have you ever done that, picturing ways of getting even with someone? Unforgiveness only hurts the one holding on to the anger and hatred. It has no affect on the one you are angry with. It is like taking poison and hoping the person you are angry with dies. Instead of seeking vengeance, Joseph trusted God and made the best of the situation he found himself in. As a result,

"the Lord was with him, and the Lord made everything he did successful." **Genesis 39:3**

Joseph didn't walk by sight, he walked by faith that God was sovereign and in control. We sometimes question whether God is in control when things get difficult. We need to understand that God is always in control.

Joseph was given a vision, and he believed that vision and held on to it. Matt Carter and Halim Suh state "Instead of letting his perception of God's silence convince Joseph that God was far away, he let the truth of God's promises shape his perception of God's silence."[73]

We can deal with suffering if we know that there is a purpose to it. When we see no purpose in our suffering we become discouraged and disillusioned. Satan uses difficult times in our lives to make us doubt God's goodness and love. Or he tries to make us believe that they are the result of sin in our lives. He is called "the accuser of the brethern" see **Revelation 12:10**

Application

How do you respond when things go wrong in your life? Do you complain, get discouraged, stay strong, feel like quitting, pray?

Have you ever been punished for doing the right thing?

Have you ever been falsely accused? How did you respond?

WEEK TEN

Day 1

Genesis 40 Joseph Interprets Dreams of Cupbearer and Baker

Observation

1. a. Who was Pharaoh angry with?
   b. What did Pharaoh do with them?

2. What did Joseph notice about his charges?

3. Describe the dreams of the cupbearer and the baker.

4. Who does Joseph say interpretations of dreams belongs to?

5. What request does Joseph make?

6. What statement does Joseph make concerning his situation?

7. What does Joseph say is the interpretation of the dreams?

8. What happened on Pharaoh's birthday?

9. What did the cupbearer do?

Correlation

A. *Encouraging Others*
    1. What are we told concerning encouraging others in **2 Corinthians 1:4**.

B. *Responding to Trials*
    2. What are we told in **James 1:2-4** concerning how we are to respond to trials in our lives?

C. *Proper Service*
    3. What does **Colossians 3:24-25** instruct us about how we are to serve?

Commentary

vs 1 The cupbearer and baker were positions that protected the king's food from being poisoned. They tasted the food and drink before it was given to the king.

vs 4 Here we see that "the captain of the guard" who apparently was Pontiphar-see **Gen 39:1**, again entrusted Joseph with important prisoners.

vs 6-7 Joseph wasn't self-absorbed in his own problems. He noticed and inquired about why Pharaoh's officers were sad. He didn't complain about his own situation. We are told in **James 1:2** that we are to respond to trials we face with "pure joy" because it is a testing of our faith and develops perseverance. To persevere is to persist in spite of negative influences, opposition, or discouragement. Joy means to have a deep sense of peace in painful situations being confident that God is in control and will never leave us. Difficult experiences can strengthen us. Enduring through difficult situations helps us to become more mature.

vs 14 This is the only record of Joseph asking anyone for any assistance.

vs 19 Joseph isn't subtle and he doesn't mince words with his interpretation.

vs 23 At this point, Joseph was 28 years old-see **41:1,46**. We don't know how long he has been in prison.

Application

Are you guilty of getting self-absorbed in your own problems and fail to be concerned about others? Do you notice when people around you are sad and discouraged? Do you try to offer comfort and encouragement?

When have you been forgotten? When have you been guilty of forgetting someone?

Genesis 41 Pharaoh's Dreams
Observation

1. How much time passes since the incident with the cupbearer and baker?

2. What happens at this point to Pharaoh?

3. Describe the dreams of Pharaoh.

4. a. What does Pharaoh do?
   b. What is the result?

5. What does the cupbearer tell Pharaoh?

6. What does Pharaoh do?

7. Who does Joseph say will give Pharoah the interpretation?

8. What does Joseph say is the interpretation of the dreams?

9. What does Joseph tell Pharaoh in **vs 32**?

10. What four step suggestion does Joseph make to Pharaoh?

11. What does Pharaoh say about Joseph?

12. What does Pharaoh do?

13. What does Pharaoh give to Joseph?

14. Who was the priest of On?

15. Who became Joseph's wife?

16. What new name is given to Joseph?

17. a. What were the names of Joseph's two sons?
    b. What did their names mean?

18. How old is Joseph at this point?

Correlation

What does **Acts 7:10** tell us about this event?
What are we told in **Psalm 105:20-22** tell us about these events?

Commentary

vs 1 Another two years pass for Joseph in prison. Might he have been discouraged and believe he would never get out? He is in a period of waiting. It is dangerous to run ahead of God. Waiting can be one of the hardest things for a person to do. It can make us feel as if we have been forgotten. When David felt that the Lord had forgotten him, he cried out.

How long will You forget me O Lord? Forever? How long will You hide Your face from me? Psalm 13:1

> **vs 9** Had the cupbearer really forgotten-that would imply he was ungrateful for what Joseph had done. Did the cupbearer use this as an opportunity to make himself look good?

vs 14 The fact that Pharaoh was willing to seek help from a foreign prisoner indicates just how desperate Pharaoh was. How do you think Joseph felt to be summoned before Pharaoh? Scared, excited? How would you feel to be summoned to meet with the president?

vs 15 Suppose Joseph had become bitter toward the cupbearer and refused to interpret Pharaoh's dream.

Joseph's reputation preceded him. What would others say about you.

vs 16 Joseph does not take any credit, stating "It is not in me". Joseph gave God the credit for interpreting the dreams. Remember that Pharaoh was considered a god in the Egyptian religion. Joseph was stating that the Lord was superior and sovereign over Pharaoh and the gods of Egypt. He was taking a big chance. We also should always be ready to declare the Lord to others.

but sanctify the Lord God in your hearts: and be ready always to give an answer to every man that asketh you a reason of the hope that is in you with meekness and fear: *1 Peter 3:15*

> Joseph could have chosen to flatter Pharaoh and try to impress him, but he didn't do that.

I find it interesting that Joseph was so willing to interpret Pharaoh's dream. Joseph himself had dreamed a double dream, and it had not come to pass. If anything, the exact opposite had occurred. Joseph may have considered the possibility that Pharaoh would be angered by the interpretation.

vs 38 Pharaoh recognized that Joseph had the Spirit of God upon him. How would the pagan realize this? Because Joseph didn't try to impress him. There was no way that Pharaoh could know for sure that Joseph's interpretation was correct. Recall that in **vs 16** Joseph had stated that God would give Pharaoh an "answer of peace". When Pharaoh heard Joseph's interpretation his heart had peace and was confident that Joseph's interpretation was correct.

We must not attempt to exalt ourselves, but wait for the Lord to exalt us.

At this point, Joseph was an ambassador for God. We are also ambassadors for Christ. **2 Corinthians 5:20** Now then we are ambassadors for Christ...

vs 40 How radical for Pharaoh to put a foreigner in second-in-command of his country.

vs 45 Joseph's new name-Zaphenath-Paneah may mean "God speaks, he lives", or "a revealer of secrets".

Asenath may mean "belonging to Neith".

On was a center for sun worship that came to be known as Heliopolis which means sun city.[74]

vs 46 Joseph was 17 when he was sold by his brothers-**37:2**. Thirteen years have passed.

vs 50-52 Joseph has two sons-Manasseh means forget; Ephraim means twice fruitful. God's blessings cause us to forget our troubles. The first name focuses on a God who perseveres. The second name focuses on a God who blesses. Both names are testimony to God's faithfulness.

SUMMARY

Joseph is a prime example of what Peter instructs us to do.

Humble yourselves therefore under the mighty hand of God, that he may exalt you in due time: 7 casting all your care upon him; for he careth for you. We need to depend on God's timing and depend on Him to exalt us. *1 Peter 5:6-7*

DAY 2

GENESIS 42 JOSEPH'S BROTHERS IN EGYPT

Observation

1. What does Jacob say to his sons?

2. How many of his sons did Jacob send to Egypt?

3. a. Which son did not go?
   b. Why did he not go?

4. Who sold grain to the people?

5. What did Joseph's brothers do when they arrived?

6. What two things did Joseph do when he saw his brothers?

7. a. What did he ask them?
   b. What answer do they give?

8. a. What does Joseph then accuse them of?
   b. What is their reply to this?

9. What test does Joseph propose?

10. What does Joseph state on the third day?

11. What does Joesph tell his brothers they must do?

12. What is the response of the brothers to their situation?

13. What does Reuben say?

14. What do the brothers not realize?

15. What is Joseph's response to what his brothers say?

16. What three orders does Joseph give?

17. What is the reaction of the brothers when one of the brothers discover that their silver had been returned?

18. What is Jacob's reaction when he is told what happened in Egypt?

19. What does Reuben say?

20. What is Jacob's response?

Correlation

1. What does **Acts 7:11-12** tell us?

Commentary

vs 6 Here Joseph's dreams are fulfilled. He is about 37 or 38 at this time.

vs 21 Here we are told how Joseph reacted when his brothers sold him.

vs 22 See **Genesis 37:21-22**

vs 24 Here we see Joseph's tender heart.

Joseph is in total control of his brothers at this point. They were at his mercy. He could have sought revenge. Could God have been testing Joseph at this point?

Why did Joseph choose Simeon to be held as prisoner? During the brothers discussion of their guilt, Joseph heard for the first time that Reuben, the firstborn had kept the brothers from killing Joseph. Joseph may have then chosen Simeon, the second oldest. Simeon may have instigated the other brothers to kill Joseph. Remember Simeon had been involved in the slaughter of the Shechemites.

vs 28 Why did Joseph return the brothers silver? Remember that they had sold him for 20 pieces of silver. The brothers may have thought that they got away with what they had done. Based on their statements the brothers may have felt guilty all these years. **Numbers 32:23** tells us to "be sure your sin will find you out".

vs 38 "He is the only one left" Imagine how this statement must have made the brothers feel. Did Jacob not care about them at all?

Vocabulary

vs 6 bowed down-*shachah*-means to prostrate oneself as if to pay homage to royalty or God.[75]

vs 10 lord-*adown*-means "sovereign" or "controller".[76]

Day 3

Genesis 43 The Second Journey Down to Egypt

Observation

1. What did Jacob say to his sons when they had eaten all the grain?

2. What did Judah say to Jacob?

3. What did Jacob ask?

4. a. What did the brothers answer?
   b. What two questions had Joseph asked?

5. What did Judah say?

6. What instructions did Jacob give his sons?

7. What was Jacob's prayer?

8. What instructions did Joseph give to his steward?

9. a. Where were the brothers taken?
   b. What did the brothers think?

10. What did the brothers do?

11. What were they told?

12. What did the steward do?

13. When was Joseph to arrive?

14. What did the brothers do when Joseph came home?

15. What three questions did Joseph ask them?

16. What did the brothers do?

17. What did Joseph say to Benjamin?

18. What did Joseph do after seeing his brother?

19. a. What was the eating arrangement?
    b. What was the reason for this?

20. What order were the brothers seated?

21. How big was Benjamin's portion?

Commentary

vs 11 Jacob again tries to manipulate the situation. He once again resorts to trying to gain good will by giving gifts as a strategy of diplomacy.

vs 16, 34 The feast was a celebration as well as a test. Benjamin was given a larger portion than the rest of the brothers to see what the reaction of the other brothers would be.

vs 26 These items from Joseph's home country may have been items which Joseph may not have had since he was in Egypt.

vs 28 This is another fulfillment of Joseph's dream.

vs 29 Benjamin at this point would be at least 21. Joseph has been in Egypt for at least 21 years. He was 17 when his brothers sold him.**37:2** He was 30 when he became second in command over Egypt. **41:46** The seven years of plenty have passed.

vs 30 Mixed emotions cause Joseph to weep. He was joyful at seeing his full blooded brother again, and sorrowful at all the lost years of fellowship.

Food for Thought

vs 33 Henry Morris states "There are no less than 39,917,000 different orders in which eleven individuals could have been seated".[77]

Day 4

Genesis 44 The Silver Cup

Observation

1. What instructions does Joseph give to his steward?

2. What did Joseph have his steward do shortly after his brothers left?

3. What did Joseph instruct the steward to say?

4. What was the cup used for?

5. What was the response of the brothers when the steward made the accusation?

6. What did the brothers say would be the consequence if the cup was found among them?

7. What order did the steward search the sacks?

8. Whose sack was the cup found in?

9. What was the reaction of the brothers when the cup was found?

10. What did the brothers do when they were in front of Joseph?

11. What questions did Joseph ask the brothers?

12. What questions did Reuben respond with?

13. What does Reuben state?

14. What is Joseph's response?

15. What does Judah state about Joseph?

16. What does Judah say would happen if Benjamin did not return to his father?

17. What does Judah offer to do?

18. Mark all the times Judah mentions his father in **vs 18-34**.

Correaltion

1. What does **Acts 7:13-14** tell us about these events?

Commentary

In this account, Joseph sets up Benjamin to make it look like he had stolen his silver cup. He did this to test the brothers and see if they would abandon him. Joseph has the chance to seek revenge against his brothers, but instead he desires reconcilliation. But he first tests them to see if their hearts have changed over the years.

vs 9 Here we see the danger of making rash vows.

vs 14 Here is yet another fulfillment of Joseph's dream.

vs 18-34 Compare this with Judah's treatment of Joseph in **Genesis 37:26-27**. The fate which Judah had sentenced Joseph is now the fate he himself is faced with.

Judah mentions his father fourteen times.

From this speech we see that Judah has changed from one who sold his brother as a slave to one who is now willing to be a slave in the place of his brother.

Day 5

Genesis 45 Joseph Makes Himself Known

Observation

1. What instructions does Joseph give?

2. a. What does Joseph do?
   b. Who heard him?

3. What is the reaction of the brothers?

4. What encouragement does Joseph give to his brothers?

5. a. What was Joseph's perspective about why he was in Egypt?
   b. Who did he say was the one who had sent him to Egypt?

6. How long has the famine been in the land at this point?

7. What instructions does Joseph give to his brothers?

8. What promises does Joseph make here?

9. What did Joseph say would happen otherwise?

10. What does Joseph tell his brothers to tell his father?

11. What did Joseph do with his brother Benjamin?

12. What does he do with his brothers?

13. What was Pharaoh's reaction when he heard Joseph's brothers had come?

14. What offer does he make?

15. What were the brothers given to bring back their families?

16. a. What were they told not to bother with?
    b. Why were they not to do this?

17. What did Joseph give to each of his brothers?

18. What did he give to his brother Benjamin?

19. What did Joseph say to his brothers as they were leaving?

20. What did the brothers say to Jacob?

21. What was Jacob's reaction?

22. What does Jacob say he will do?

Correlation

A. *Forgiveness*
   1. What are we instructed to get rid of in **Ephesians 4:31**?

   2. What are we told to do in **Ephesians 4:32**?

   3. What did Jesus say concerning forgiveness in **Matthew 18:21-22**?

   4. What did Jesus say we were to do if we were making an offering and remember that our brother had something against us? See **Matthew 5:23-24**

B. *Revenge*
   1. What are we instructed in **Romans 12:17**?

2. Who according to **Romans 12:19** has the right to revenge?

3. a. What are we instructed in **Proverbs 25:21-22** to do to our enemies?
   b. What will this result in?

4. What are we told in **Leviticus 19:18** concerning revenge?

Commentary

vs 5,7,9 Four times Joseph states that God-not his brothers was the one who was responsible for what had happened. This is Joseph's secret to not desiring to seek revenge.

God has a plan and purpose for everyone's life.

Choosing to forgive someone brings peace to your heart and soul. Being angry gives the other person control over our thoughts and emotions. Forgiveness isn't easy, but it is a choice. Remember all the offenses we are guilty of and which God has forgiven us of.

> And forgive us our debts, as we forgive our debtors. *Matthew 6:12*

> Corrie ten Boom said "Forgiveness is the key which unlocks the door of resentment and the handcuffs of hatred. It breaks the chains of bitterness and the shackles of selfishness."[78]

vs 26 The Bible does not record that the brothers ever tell Jacob what they had done to Joseph. I wonder if they ever did tell Jacob.

Application

Who do you need to forgive?

Is there someone from whom you need to seek forgiveness?

WEEK ELEVEN

Day 1

Genesis 46 Jacob Goes to Egypt

Observation

1. a. Where does Jacob stop?
   b. What does he do there?

2. a. Who speaks to Jacob?
   b. How does he communicate with Jacob?
   c. What does he say?

3. How many sons did Reuben have?

4. How many sons did Simeon have?

5. How many sons did Levi have?

6. a. How many sons did Judah have?
   b. Who died in Canaan?

7. How many sons did Judah's son Perez have?

8. How many sons did Issachar have?

9. How many sons did Zebulun have?

10. How many sons did Gad have?

11. a. How many sons did Asher have?
    b. Who was their sister?

12. How many sons did Asher's son Beriah have?

13. Who were the sons of Joseph?

14. How many sons did Benjamin have?

15. Who was the son of Dan?

16. How many sons did Naphtali have?

17. What was the total number of Jacob's family who went to Egypt?

18. What did Jacob do before arriving in Egypt?

19. What instructions does Joseph give to his brothers?

20. What do we learn about the Egyptians?

Correlation

1. What are we told about who came to Egypt with Jacob in the following verses?
   Exodus 1:5
   Acts 7:14

Commentary

vs 1 Jacob offers sacrifices in Beersheba.

vs 2 This is Jacob's seventh encounter with the Lord.

vs 6 Jacob took all of his possessions with him even though Pharoah tells them not to be concerned with them. Jacob did not want to be dependent upon anyone but the Lord.

vs 8-27 Here we are given a list of Jacob's descendants who go to Egypt with him. The total is 70 people.

vs 29-30 Joseph is reunited with his father. Jacob is 130 at this point. Joseph had last seen his father when he was 17. Joseph is now 39. Twenty-two long years have passed.

Day 2

Genesis 47 Jacob in Egypt

Observation

1. What did Joseph tell Pharaoh?

2. What does Pharaoh ask the brothers?

3. What did the brothers respond?

4. What does Pharaoh instruct Joseph to do?

5. What does Jacob do when he meets Pharaoh?

6. What does Pharaoh ask Jacob?

7. What does Joseph first sell corn for?

8. After this ran out, what did he next take in exchange for bread?

9. a. After this also ran out, what did Joseph then take for food?
    b. Who was exempt from this?
    c. Why were they exempt?

10. What arrangement did Joseph make with the people?

11. a. Where did the Israelites settle?
    b. What was the conditon of the Israelites?

12. How long did Jacob live in Egypt?

13. How old was Jacob?

14. What request did Jacob make of Joseph?

15. What did Jacob do?

Commentary

vs 7, 10 Jacob blesses Pharaoh when he entered and when he left Pharaoh. God had told Abraham that He would "bless those who bless you" **Genesis 12:3**. So Pharaoh is now blessed by God through Jacob.

vs 14-21 Joseph collected all the money in the land, then all the livestock, and then all the land. There was no welfare system. Food was not given for nothing. There was no welfare system. The Bible says that if a man doesn't work he shouldn't eat. See **2 Thessalonians 3:10**.

vs 28 Jacob was in Egypt for 17 years. Joseph would now be 56 years old.

Day 3

Genesis 48 Jacob Blesses Manasseh and Ephraim

Observation
___

1. What was Joseph told?

2. What did Joseph do?

3. What name did Jacob call the Lord?

4. What did Jacob say the Lord had told him?

5. What are we told about Jacob in **vs 10**?

6. What did Jacob do with Joseph's sons?

7. What blessing does Jacob give in **vs 16**?

8. What did Joseph do?

9. What did Jacob do when blessing Joseph's sons?

10. What testimony did Jacob give concerning the Lord?

11. What did Joseph do?

12. What was Jacob's response?

13. What prophesy did Jacob make about what God would do?

14. What did Jacob give to Joseph?

Correlation

1. What did the Lord tell Abraham in **Gen 12:2-3; 17:5-8**?

2. What are we told about this event in **Hebrews 11:21**?

Commentary

vs 1 Joseph's sons would have been in their twenties at this point. They were born before the beginning of the famine-see **Genesis 41:50-52**. Jacob came to Egypt in the second year of the famine-see **Genesis 45:6**. At that point Jacob was 130-see **Genesis 47:9** and he had lived in Egypt 17 years, dying at the age of 147. See **Genesis 47:28**.

vs 19-20 Here yet again the younger is put before the older.

Day 4

Genesis 49 Jacob Blesses His Sons

Observation

1. What did Jacob say concerning Reuben?

2. What did he say concerning Simeon and Levi?

3. To what animal did Jacob associate with the tribe of Judah?

4. What did Jacob say would not depart from Judah?

5. Where did Jacob say Zebulun would live?

6. What would Zebulun become a haven for?

7. What animal does Jacob associate Issachar with?

8. What does Jacob say Issachar would submit to?

9. What would Dan provide for his people?

10. What animal does Jacob associate with Dan?

11. What does Jacob state he looks for?

12. a. What would happen to Gad?
    b. What would Gad do in return?

13. What is said about Asher?

14. What animal is Naphtali associated with?

15. To what does Jacob compare Joseph?

16. What four different names does Jacob use to refer to God?

17. What two actions does Jacob say the Lord does?

18. What three blessings does Jacob bestow on Joseph?

19. What animal does Jacob associate with Benjamin?

20. What instructions does Jacob give concerning his burial?

21. Who had been buried in the cave?

Correlation

1. What are we told about concerning Reuben in **Genesi 35:22; 1 Chronicles 5:1-2**?

Commentary

vs 5 This refers to the brothers slaughtering the Shechemites because their leader had defiled their sister Dinah. See **Gen 34**.

The tribe of Levi became priests of Israel through using their swords-this time for God. See **Exodus 32:27-29**.

vs 7 Levi became the priestly tribe, and as such never received an inheritance of land.

vs 9-10 This is a Messianic prophecy. From the tribe of Judah came King David and was the tribe from which Jesus was descended.

In **Revelation 5:5** Jesus is referred to as the lion from the tribe of Judah.

Scepter- symbol of rule

*Shiloh-*Means peaceful one. It was where the tabernacle was set up. It also referred to the Lord and promised Savior.

shel and *loh* means "to whom it belongs".

vs 31 Leah's death is not recorded, but here we learn that she and not Jacob's beloved Rachel is buried in the family sepulcher.

Jacob Summary

Jacob was a very passive person as seen when his daughter Dinah was raped (**Gen 34:5**), when his sons Simeon and Levi slaughtered the Shechemites (**34:30**) and when his son Reuben went into his concubine Billah and slept with her (**Gen 35:22**).

He had numerous encounters with the Lord.
1. **Genesis 28:12-17** Bethel on way to Padan-aram

2. **Genesis 31:3** The Lord instructs Jacob to return to the land of his fathers.

3. **Genesis 31:10-13** a dream telling him to return to his homeland.

4. **Genesis 32:24-32** wrestled with the Lord. Name changed to Israel.

5. **Genesis 35:1** Instructs Jacob to go to Bethel. This was where Jacob had first encountered the Lord.

6. **Genesis 46:2-4** The Lord appears to Jacob at Beersheba as Jacob went to Egypt to be reunited with his son Joseph.

JACOB'S TRAVELS

Beersheba **Genesis 28:10**

Padan-aram (Haran) **Genesis 28:5,10**

Succoth **Genesis 33:17**

Shechem **Genesis 33:18**

Bethel **Genesis 35:6**

Migdal Eder **Genesis 31:21**

Mamre, Kiriath Arba (Hebron) **Genesis 35:27**

Valley of Hebron **Genesis 37:14**

Goshen (Egypt) **Genesis 46:6,28**

Jacob's Timeline

Joseph born 91

Joseph sold by his brothers 108

Isaac his father dies when Jacob is 120 years old. He had been 60 years old when Jacob was born see **Genesis 25:26.**

Jacob came to Egypt when he is 130. See **Genesis 47:9** Joseph has been in Egypt for 22 years. This is the second year of the famine. See **Genesis 45:6**

Jacob dies at the age of 147. See **Genesis 47:28**

Day 5

Genesis 50 The Death of Jacob and Joseph

Observation

1. What three things did Joseph do when his father died?

2. a. What instructions does Joseph give?
   b. To whom does he give these instructions?
   c. How long did the process take?

3. What request does Joseph make of Pharaoh?

4. Who accompanied Joseph?

5. Who of Joseph's relatives were left in Goshen?

6. a. Where did Joseph observe a seven-day period of mourning?
   b. What did the Canaanites call the place?

7. What concern did Joseph's brother's have?

8. a. What do Joseph's brother's do?
   b. What is Joseph's reaction?

9. a. What do Joseph's brother's do next?
   b. What does Joseph say to them?
   c. What does Joseph acknowledge about his brothers intentions?
   d. What does Joseph say was God's purpose?

10. How old was Joseph when he died?

11. What two things did Joseph say that God would do?

Correlation

1. Where was Joseph buried? See **Joshua 24:32**.

2. What are we told about Joseph in **Hebrews 11:22**?

3. How are we to repay evil according to **Hebrews 12:21**?

Commentary

vs 15-21 This was seventeen years after Joseph had made himself known to his brothers! They have been holding this guilt all this time. Jacob makes no mention in his blessing of what the brothers did to Joseph. They may never have told him what they had done. There is no record of them confessing to Jacob. Joseph did not tell them to tell Jacob what they had done when they went to get Jacob- see **45:4-11**. Joseph would probably want to have spared his father additional pain. Imagine how God feels when He has forgiven and forgotten our confessed sins and we keep going back and asking for forgiveness again.

I, even I, am he that blotteth out thy transgressions for mine own sake, and will not remember thy sins. *Isaiah 43:25*

And they shall teach no more every man his neighbour, and every man his brother, saying, Know the Lord: for they shall all know me, from the least of them unto the greatest of them, saith the Lord: for I will forgive their iniquity, and I will remember their sin no more. *Jeremiah 31:34*

vs 22 Joseph was 56 when his father died. He dies at the age of 110. He has been in Egypt since he was 17 years old.

Summary of Joseph

Here is a man who didn't let his circumstances dictate how he would react. He chose to live a life of integrity and instead of being resentful and seeking revenge agaist those who had wronged him, he chose to forgive.He was a man who had been wronged, yet instead of becoming hardened and bitter he was sensitive toward others, even those who had wronged him. We see him weeping many times, but never because of his circumstances. He never felt sorry for himself.

Joseph's Timeline

17 Sold by his brothers **Genesis 37:2**

30 Becomes vizier of Egypt 30-37 Two sons born

39 Father comes to Egypt See **Genesis 47:9**

56 His father dies **Genesis 47:28**

110 Joseph dies **Genesis 50:22, 26**

Parallels Between Joseph and Jesus

Joseph		Jesus
37:3	Both were loved by their fathers	Matthew 3:17
37:2	Both were shepherds of their father's sheep	John 10:11,27
37:13-14	Both were sent by their fathers to their brothers	Hebrews 2:11
37:4	Both were hated by their brothers	John 7:5
37:20	Both were plotted against by others	John 11:53
39:7-10	Both experienced severe temptation	Matthew 4:1-10
37:25	Both were taken to Egypt	Matthew 2:14-15
37:23	Both were stripped of their robes	John 19:23
37:28	Both were sold for the price of a slave	Matthew 26:15
Psalm 105:17-18	Both were bound in chains	Matthew 27:2
39:16-18	Both were falsely accused	Matthew 26:59-60
40:2-3	Both were involved with two other prisoners one of which was saved and the other lost	Luke 23:32
41:46	Both were publicly recognized at age 30	Luke 3:23
41:	Both were exalted after suffering	Philippians 2:9-11
45:1-15	Both forgave those who wronged them	Luke 23:34
45:7	Both saved peoples lives	Matthew 1:21

SUMMARY

In Genesis we see God as Creator, Redeemer, Provider and Leader. In this book we meet regular people who face difficulties in life just as we all do today. We encounter God as He interacts with people. We see that He judges sin, but that He is also merciful. He is faithful even when we are unfaithful.

Names of God found in Genesis

Name	Meaning of name	Reference
Elohim	God	Chapter 1
Yahweh	Lord God	Chapter 2
El Elyon	God Most High	15:14
El Roi	The One Who Sees Me	16:13
El Shaddai	God Almighty The Lord, the Eternal God	17:1; 28:3; 35:11; 43:14 21:33
Jehovah Jira	The Lord Will Provide The Fear of Isaac	22:14 31:42, 53
El Elohe Israel	God of Isreal or Mighty is the God of Israel	33:20
El Bethel	God of Bethel	35:7
Mighty One of Jacob		49:24
The Shepherd		49:24
The Rock of Israel		49:24
Shaddai	The Almighty	49:25

Character Quiz

Match the names in the left column with left column

A. Adam	1. Never died
B. Eve	2. Offered as a sacrifice by his father
C. Cain	3. Daughter of Jacob
D. Able	4. Became second in command of Egypt
E. Seth	5. First woman
F. Enoch	6. Mother of Ishmael
G. Noah	7. Slept with his daughter-in-law
H. Canaan	8. Was hanged by Pharaoh
I. Abram	9. Sold his birthright for a bowl of stew
J. Sarah	10. Named all the animals
K. Ishmael	11. Had two disturbing dreams
L. Hagar	12. Was a preacher of righteousness
M. Isaac	13. Mother of Joseph
N. Rebekah	14. Third son of Adam and Eve
O. Esau	15. Wife of Joseph
P. Jacob	16. Abraham's son through Sarah's maid
Q. Laban	17. Killed by his brother
R. Rachel	18. Forgot about Joseph
S. Leah	19. Father of 12 sons
T. Dinah	20. Mother at age of 90
U. Judah	21. Laban's older daughter
V. Joseph	22. Son cursed by his father
W. Pharaoh	23. Wife of Jacob
X. chief baker	24. First murderer
Y. Chief cupbearer	25. Deceived Jacob
Z. Asenath	26. Given promise of many descendants

BIBLIOGRAPHY

1 David W. Cloud, *Genesis Advanced Bible Study Series* (Port Huron, Mi: Way of Life Literature, 2004) 35-36

2 ibid 49

3 ibid 51

4 Anne Graham Lotz, *God's Story* (Nashville:Word Publishing, 1997) xxiv

5 Jack W. Hayford, *Genesis Promises and Beginnings* (Nashville: Thomas Nelson, 2009) xiii

6 Matthew Henry, *Matthew Henry's Commentary on the Whole Bible* (USA: Hendrickson Publishers, 1991) Vol 1

7 Jack W. Hayford *Genesis Promises and Beginnings*, 13

8 *HCSB Study Bible* (Nashville:Holman Bible Publishers, 2010)16
9 ibid 17

10 ibid 17

11 Hayford, *Genesis Promises and Beginnings*, 26

12 Matt Carter and Halim Suk, *Creation Unraveled* (Nashville: Lifeway Publishers 2011) 92

13 John H Walton, *The NIV Application Commentary: Genesis* (Grand Rapids, Mich: Zondervan, 2001) 338

14 James Montgomery Boice, *Genesis Volume 1: Creation and Fall* (Grand Rapids, Mich: Baker Books 1998, 327

15 Henry H. Halley, *Halley's Bible Handbook Classic Edition* (Grand Rapids, Mi:Zondervan, 1927, 24th ed. 1965)75

16 ibid 76

17 ibid 77

18 ibid 76-77

19 David Atkinson *The Message of Genesis 1-11* (Downers Grove: Intervarsity Press, 1990) 178

20 *HCSB Study Bible*, 28

21 Lawrence O Richards, *The Revell Bible Dictionary* (New York: Wynward Press, 1990)119

22 ibid 1002

23 Warren W. Wiersbe, General Editor, *The Transformation Study Bible* (Colorado Springs, Co: David C. Cook, 2009) 25

24 Halley, *Halley's Bible Handbook Classic Edition*, 85

25 Wiersby, *The Transformation Study Bible* 27

26 Larry Richards, General Editor, *The Book of Genesis, The Smart Guide to the Bible Series*, (Nashville, Tenn: Nelson Books, 2007) 115

27 Anne Graham Lotz *Magnificent Obsession* (Grand Rapids, Mi: Zondervan 2009) 269

28 Hayford, *Genesis Promises and Beginnings*, 48

29 John MacArthur, *The Father of Israel, Trusting God's Promises*, (Nashville, Tenn: Thomas Nelson, 2008) 108

30 Hayford, *Genesis Promises and Beginnings*, 1

31 Leslie Brown, Editor, *The Shorter Oxford English Dictionary*, (Oxford: Clarendon Press) 1993

32 Hayford, *Genesis Promises and Beginnings*, 52

33 Gene a Getz, *Abraham: Holding Fast to the Will of God* (Nashville, Tenn: Broadman and Holman Publishers, 1996) 99

34 F.B. Meyer, *Life of Abraham* (Linwood: Emerson Books, 1996) 99

35 Ray C. Steadman, *Friend of God The Legacy of Abraham, Man of Faith* (Grand Rapids, Michigan: Discovery House Publishers 2010) 104

36 Gene Wilkes, *Life Essential Study Bible*, (Nashville, Tenn:Holman Bible Publishers 2011) 25

37 ibid 24

38 Hayford, *Genesis Promises and Beginnings*, 55

39 Tremper Longman, *Genesis Thru Numbers*, (Uhrichville, Ohio:Barbour Publishing, 2009) 40

40 John MacArthur, *Father of Israel, Trusting God's Promises*, 59

41 Wayne A Barber, Eddie Rasnake, Richard l. Shepherd, *Life Principles From the Women of the Bible Book Two* (Chatanooga Tn: AMG Publishers 2002) 25

42 Cloud, *Genesis Advanced Bible Study Series*, 210-211

43 Hayford, *Promises and Beginnings*, 84

44 Sean A. Harrison, *Genesis See Our Story Begin NLT Study Series* (Carol Stream, Illinios: Tyndale House Publishers) 58

45 Benajah Harvey Carroll, *An Interpretation of the English Bible*

46 Wiersby, *The Transformation Study Bible*, 40

47 *HCSB Study Bible* 45

48 Wiersby, *The Transformation Study Bible*, 41

49 James Sidlow Baxter, *Explore the Book* (Grand Rapids, Mich: Zondervan, 1960)

50 Harrison, *Genesis See Our Story Begin NLT Study Series*, 64

51 Sarah Buswell, *Responding to God's Call* Grand Rapids Mich: Baker Books 1993) 20-21

52 Harrison, *Genesis See Our Story Begin NLT Study Series*, 64

53 Walton, *NIVAC: Genesis*, 517-518

54 Amy Carmichael, *Whispers of His Power*, (Fort Washington: Christian Literature Crusade 1982) 45

Isaac

55 Harrison, *Genesis See Our Story Begin NLT Study Series*, 66

56 Lockyer, Herbert, *All the Women of the Bible*, (Grand Rapids Michigan: Zondervan 1967) 135

57 Steidman, *Friend of God The Legacy of Abraham, Man of Faith*, 210

58 Hayford, *Genesis Promises and Beginnings*, 66

59 HCSB Study Bible, 52

60 Wiersby, *Transformation Study Bible*, 71

Jacob

61 Live Relationally 184

62 Harrison, *Genesis See Our Story Begin NLT Study Series*, 81

63 ibid, 81

64 ibid 86

65 Wirsby, *Transformation Study Bible*, 65

66 Wiersby, Warren, *Nelson's Quick Refence Chapter-by-Chapter Bible Commentary* (Nashville Tenn: Thomas Nelson 1991) 38

67 Gien Karsen, *Her Name is Woman*, (Colorado Spring Co: Nav Press 1975) 53

JOSEPH

68 Murphy, Mary Englund, Joseph Beyond the Coat of Many Colors (Canada, AMG Publishers 2011) 43

69 Longman, Tremper Quick Notes Genesis Th ru Numbers (Urickville, Ohio: Barbour Publishing 2009) 69-70

70 Mac Arthur, *Jacob and Egypt*( ) 97

71 C. S. Lewis, *The Problem of Pain* (New York: Harper Collins, 1996) 91

72 Carter, Matt; Suh, Halim, *Creation Restored, The Godpel According to Genesis* (Nashville Tenn: Lifeway Press 2012) 101
73 ibid 107

74 Harrison, *Genesis See our Story Begin*, 101

75 Murphy, *Joseph Beyond the Coat of Many Colors*, 149

76 ibid 150
77 Henry M. Morris, *The Genesis Record* (Grand Rapids, Mi: Baker Book House, 1979), 610

78 Corrie ten Boom, *Tramp for the Lord* (Fort Washington, PA:CLC Publications, 2008), 197

www.ingramcontent.com/pod-product-compliance
Lightning Source LLC
Chambersburg PA
CBHW071954070526
44583CB00015B/1194